SBN 3
Copyr
Publis e,
Queer
Made
Purnel
Londo

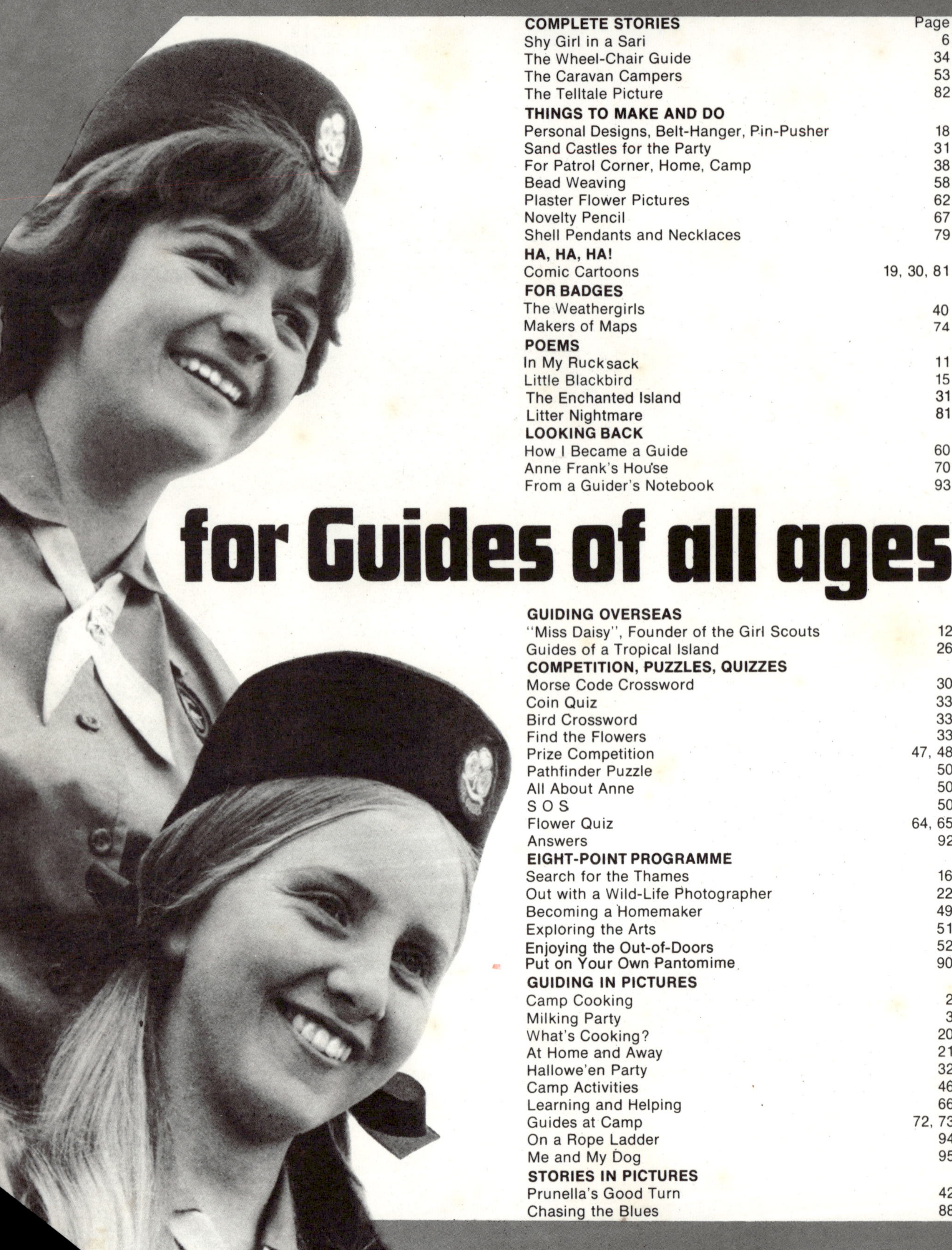

for Guides of all ages

Photos: The Croydon Advertiser.

the GIRL GUIDE annual

Published by special arrangement with
THE GIRL GUIDES ASSOCIATION

PURNELL

Shy Girl in a Sari

by Anne Lindsay

It was quite safe to plan a picnic. It wouldn't rain for months yet, for this was India in the hot weather. The Guide Guider, Miss Rose, had sprung a surprise on her Company.

"We're going for a picnic on Saturday," she said. "The bus will come for us at eleven o'clock, and we won't be back till about six."

"Oh, good!" shouted Martha, one of the Patrol Leaders.

The Guides all looked smart in their navy-blue saris and fresh white blouses. The silver border of trefoils on the saris was most attractive, and the girls themselves looked nice. Many of them had neat black pigtails and bright-brown eyes.

"Where are we going, Rosy?" asked Martha, "Rosy" being the name the Guides had bestowed on their Guider with her permission.

"That's my secret," replied the Guider. "What will you want to take with you to eat?"

"Cold curry and rice," replied Martha, without hesitation. She was a very capable Guide, with a neat, athletic figure. "We'll wrap it in some cloth and it will be easy to carry. There are some odds-and-ends left over from the dressmaking class. We can wash them and use them."

The Guider secretly promised herself that, much as she liked curry, she would not enjoy it under such conditions. There would be ordinary sandwiches for her.

The Guides all looked smart in their navy-blue saris and fresh white blouses.

The Guides were some of a larger group of Indian village girls who were being educated at the Mission Boarding School of which Rosy was in charge. Some were at the local High School, while others were learning weaving and dressmaking.

Shanti, a new Guide, was sitting quietly. She was the youngest in the Company, and Rosy guessed she was not very happy.

"You can't tease Shanti," one of the Guides had said. "She's a baby and a spoilsport."

Even Martha, Shanti's Patrol Leader, was worried.

"Shanti makes such a fuss about everything," she said. "I don't know how she'll ever become a good Guide."

"Just leave her alone," the Guider said. "She's shy. She may learn by herself. She's come from a very difficult home. She's never had fun, and her stepmother doesn't seem to be very kind to her. This is really her home now and we must help her."

Saturday morning came at last, and the Guides were awake very early. Rosy could hear their chattering and laughing. At eleven o'clock they were all settled in the bus—all, that is, but one.

"Who's missing?" asked Rosy. "Leaders, check your Patrols!"

"It's Shanti, Rosy," said Martha. "Where can she be?"

"I saw her a few minutes ago," said Parvati, another Leader. "She was looking for some cloth. I told her to ask Sarojini in the needlework room."

Behind her were monkeys of all ages and sizes.

"I'll go and look for her, Rosy," said Martha, with a sigh, but just then a small figure came rushing out of the courtyard with a bundle in her hand. It was Shanti, with her bundle of curry and rice.

"Put your lunch in the rack and sit down quickly, Shanti," said Rosy. "We're all ready to go. What kept you?"

"I couldn't find any cloth to wrap my curry in," explained Shanti shyly.

"What have you used, then?"

"My new blouse," was the reply.

"Oh, Shanti!" Martha shouted. "You silly thing! Your blouse will be ruined."

"Never mind, Shanti," said the Guider, who saw tears in Shanti's eyes. "We'll get you some cloth tomorrow and you can make yourself another blouse."

The countryside they were passing through was flat and brown, with red-roofed houses and blossoming trees giving a little colour here and there. In the distance there were groups of tall palm-trees, looking just like huge feather dusters. Far away on the horizon was a range of blue-grey hills. The sun was very hot.

The bus jolted along the stony surface of the rough road or sometimes splashed through a stream or over a field. It was a wonderful adventure for the girls. Ahead was a clump of trees.

"We're going to have our picnic in that little wood," said Rosy. "It should be cooler there."

They were there at last. What excitement there was as they took down their bundles of curry and rice from the racks and jumped out of the bus in this unknown place! They were all laughing and shouting. Only Shanti seemed to be hanging back.

"Come on, Shanti," said Martha. "Our Patrol's gathering here. We want to keep together."

"That's right," said the Guider. "There are going to be Patrol competitions, so do keep with your Leaders. Now, when you're ready we'll go into the wood."

It was much cooler among the trees, and there were some fallen trunks of trees to sit on.

"Now," said Rosy, spreading a rug on the ground, "you can leave your lunch and other belongings here beside me. Go off in Patrols and see what interesting specimens you can find for your Patrol log-books. When I blow my whistle, come back!"

Shanti trailed along at the end of the Lotus Patrol. Rachel, a fat, jolly little Guide, waited for her. She took Shanti's arm in a friendly way, but Shanti didn't

respond.

"Oh, dear!" thought the Guider, as she looked after them. "If only Shanti would laugh and enjoy life as Rachel does. I wonder why she ever wanted to be a Guide."

But she soon forgot Shanti. She took out her knitting and concentrated on it. It was a baby's coat and the pattern was rather tricky. It took up all her attention.

It was quiet in the wood. The cries of the Guides were now far away and the occasional screech of a bright-green parrakeet flying through the trees was all that broke the stillness. Rosy had never known India so quiet. It was a noisy country.

After some time she looked at her watch. It was twelve-thirty. She'd better call the Guides back. She blew her whistle. In a few minutes the cries came nearer and she began to see the first few girls. They had heard. Soon she could distinguish them—Martha, Parvati, Rachel, and Shanti—all by herself, as usual. Rachel hadn't managed to make friends with her. Suddenly Martha stood stock-still and called out: "Rosy, I can't come back! I'm scared!"

"Scared?" said the Guider. "What of?"

"Look behind you, Rosy," called Parvati, who was usually very daring, but had stopped too.

Rosy turned round and looked. Behind her, standing in a huge semi-circle not more than ten feet away, were monkeys—monkeys of all ages and sizes—babies, mothers and fathers, grandfathers and grandmothers, all moving quietly nearer and nearer and all steadily staring at her.

She had to think very quickly. She must not seem to be afraid.

"Come along, Guides!" she said. "If you don't show fear, the monkeys won't touch you."

Martha and the other three Leaders had never disobeyed her before, but they seemed rooted to the spot. The Guider didn't know what to do next. Then a small figure moved forward. It was Shanti. She moved steadily towards Rosy. Martha just had to follow. She couldn't let Shanti go alone. Soon all the Guides, following Shanti's lead, were making their way forward.

"Let's see what you have collected!" said the Guider, in a voice that she hoped sounded calm. "We'll move over to that fallen tree, and the monkeys will soon get tired of staring at us. Just put your collection down in Patrols here. We'll see who's done best."

They were all absorbed when suddenly Parvati tugged at Rosy's sleeve.

"Look, Rosy!" she shrieked. "The monkeys are stealing our lunch."

Shanti moved steadily towards Rosy.

They were both up a tree sitting on a branch.

They all looked round. Two of the biggest monkeys darted forward and grabbed a bundle of curry and rice in their teeth. In no time they were both up a tree, sitting on a branch and looking down with a sad expression in their eyes.

"Rosy," said Martha, "it's Shanti's lunch and mine that they've stolen."

"And Shanti's is wrapped in her new blouse," said Rachel.

"We must guard the rest of the lunches," said the Guider. "Come on! Stand in front of them. Perhaps the monkeys will go away."

The two monkeys in the trees had now bitten into the bundles and were stuffing themselves with curry. Their cheeks were blown out like balloons. Suddenly a laugh rang out.

"Won't that big fat monkey look fine when he eats my curry and then puts on my blouse?" giggled Shanti.

The other Guides looked hard at her, unable to believe their ears. Then they burst out laughing too. Shanti was a sport, after all! Rosy always said that a Guide must be able to laugh at herself.

"Rosy," said Rachel, "how long do you think we'll have to stay guarding our lunch? I want to eat mine. I'm so hungry."

"Oh, it will probably be a day or two," joked the Guider. "Meantime, I'll clap my hands firmly and hope they'll go away. I find that works with most animals in India."

She clapped her hands once, twice, three times. The monkeys didn't move.

Then Shanti spoke again. She was giving the Guides surprises today.

"I think," she said thoughtfully, "there must be a temple sacred to the monkey god here. The priests and people feed the monkeys there and that is why there are so many of them. If we could see a 'holy man' he might be able to help us."

They were all standing round rather gloomily when suddenly, without a word, Shanti ran off. They watched her in surprise, and soon they saw her running up to a man in an orange robe. He had long hair and a beard. He was a Hindu holy man. Shanti must have seen him when he was a long way off. Now he was coming back with her. Suddenly he clapped his hands, just once and very gently. Immediately every monkey disappeared. The curry-eating grandfathers tore up the cloth and threw it on the ground before they left the scene.

"You'll never eat your lunch here in peace," said the holy man. "Come with me!"

He led them out of the wood to a pleasant stream beside which they would be able to have their picnic.

As they shared their lunch with Martha and Shanti, they all laughed over their adventure.

The rest of the day passed very happily. Now that the food was gone, the monkeys did not trouble them. The Guides were home before sunset.

As Rosy enjoyed a welcome bath, she couldn't help overhearing the Guides recounting their adventures to their friends in the boarding-school below.

"Shanti was so brave," Martha was saying. "She didn't mind the monkeys at all. And she had the idea of telling the holy man. You should have seen the crowds of monkeys, all behind Rosy. We were all scared, except Shanti and Rosy."

In her bath the Guider smiled privately. If they but knew!

"Shanti ought to be made a Leader," said one of the girls.

"I hope she will soon be one," said Martha. "We're proud of her."

Rosy smiled happily. There was no need to worry about Shanti now!

IN MY RUCKSACK

The soft sound of the river,
The strong sound of the sea,
The world turning over,
From June to January;
The sound of grass growing,
The wild wind in the wood.
I'd put them in my rucksack
And keep them if I could!

The old leaves changing
To yellows, reds and browns;
The young wheat fringing
The far-flung vales and downs.
The hedgerows and the ditches,
The shadows on the hill;
I put them in my rucksack
And they're in there still.

by Jean Kenward

Miss Daisy, Founder of the Girl Scouts

A two-act opera entitled "Daisy" was recently presented in the U.S.A. to commemorate Juliette Gordon Low, Founder of the Girl Scouts of America. Hundreds of Girl Scouts and their leaders attended the premiere, which presented a renowned soprano, Elizabeth Volkman, in the title role.

Mrs Juliette Low was known from childhood by the pet name of "Daisy", but it doesn't really fit her resolute character. She was born in Savannah, Georgia, in 1860. She married William Low and lived half of each year in Great Britain and half in the U.S.A.

She met the Founder of Scouting, Lord Baden-Powell, in Scotland, and decided to start a Company of Guides in a lonely Scottish valley, Glen Lyon. The cottages were so few and far apart that the Company at first numbered only seven girls, one of whom walked seven miles on a Saturday afternoon to join Mrs Low and the other new Guides at Mrs Low's house, where they not only learned about the Guide Law, knotting, flags, knitting and cooking, but enjoyed a wonderful tea too! Map-reading and signalling were taught them by a visiting Guards officer.

Mrs Low found that boys and girls living in the valley had to leave home early to earn a living somewhere else. So she taught them how to raise chickens and sell them to the shooting-lodges in the mountain, so enabling them to stay at home and earn. She had a spinning-wheel, and with this she taught the girls how to spin. The girls became so good at this craft that they were able to spin in the dark, this being a great advantage, as the cottagers were not able to afford lighting. That first year they spun twenty pounds of the wool available in their sheep-raising district. This they sold to a shop in London.

When she left Scotland to return to America, Mrs Low left her Guides in the charge of the village postmistress. On arriving in London the following summer, she heard of the big Empire Day parade that was being held in Hyde Park and learned that the Guides were to be there.

"You can't possibly get in," her friends told her, but for Juliette Low there was no such word as "can't". She got in!

At the parade she met her Guides again and learned that some of them had begun their own Companies.

In 1911 Mrs Low started more Companies in London. She paid all the expenses of the first Company, took a deep interest in every member, and looked after them all for six or seven years.

Her second Company met in a clubroom in a poor part of Lambeth, London. She soon had twenty Guides, for whom she needed a regular leader. Off she went to Mrs Mark Kerr, whom she knew only slightly but who later became a close friend.

Mrs Kerr replied that she couldn't possibly take on the Company. "I have no time," she declared. "I do not live in London, and I am no good with girls."

Mrs Low, who was deaf in one ear, turned this one to Mrs Kerr, and said sweetly, "Then that's settled! The next meeting is on Thursday, and I have told them you will take it. I sail for America next week, but I shall be back in six months' time. I will pay for the girls' uniforms and any other expenses you may be put to, and I should like you to give them a good tea every week after the meeting. Goodbye!"

Off she went, leaving the new leader gasping. But Mrs Kerr took up her duties, soon grew to love Guiding, and became prominent in the Movement.

Mrs Low often made use of her deafness to avoid hearing refusals to take part in the Movement she cared about so deeply. "I knew I could rely on you," she would say, conveniently failing to hear a regretful refusal of her invitation to form a new Company or lead one. Her deafness was a handicap to her in holding meetings, interviewing people, and interesting others in Guiding, but she never let it hinder her work for Guiding.

There is an amusing story about

her when she represented the Girl Scouts of America at a public meeting in London. One of the speakers was a lady she greatly admired and she was sorry the audience did not applaud her. So, although she could not hear what was being said, she clapped loudly and cried "Hear, hear!" every time the speaker paused for breath. It was not until afterwards that she found out that the speech had been all about herself. When the speaker said, "Mrs Low is a remarkable woman," Mrs Low had shouted out "Hear, hear!" When the speaker described the founding of the Girl Scouts of America as a marvellous piece of work by Mrs Low, Mrs Low had applauded loudly!

Mrs Low continued to travel backwards and forwards between the Girl Scouts of Savannah and the Girl Guides of London. Even after World War I began in 1914, the Guide Movement grew stronger and stronger. When Lady Baden-Powell was elected World Chief Guide in 1916, Mrs Low was asked to be Commissioner for the West Central Division of London, a post she held for some years.

When Lady Baden-Powell started the International Council of the Girl Guides and Girl Scouts, Mrs Low was elected representative for the U.S.A. She never missed a meeting when she was in Europe, and often came over from America especially for one. She would sit quietly at the table with a hearing-aid in her hand.

In 1922, Foxlease, in the New Forest, was presented to British Girl Guides by Mrs Anne Archbold of Washington, D.C. Mrs Low became active in planning the furnishings for one of the cottages. This was to be called 'The Link", in token of the friendship between the U.S.A.

Lord (then Sir Robert) Baden-Powell and Lady Baden-Powell with Juliette Low in 1919

Photos: The World Association of Girl Guides and Girl Scouts

and Britain. The money to be spent was entrusted to Mrs Low, who also painted delightful little medallions, sketches and pictures and made sculptures for it.

During the World Camp held at Foxlease in 1924, she and her devoted Scottish maid, Bella, stayed at The Link and entertained the campers to breakfast—

Juliette Low touring the World Camp in New York in 1926 with Sir Robert and Lady Baden-Powell. Mrs Low is standing left of B.-P., next to whom is Mrs Arthur Choate, her god-daughter, who is still active in American Girl Scouting today

"The Birthplace", the handsome Regency mansion in Savannah, Georgia, U.S.A., where Juliette Low was born in 1860. Threatened with demolition, the house was bought by the Girl Scouts of America in 1953 and is now filled with mementoes of the pioneer Guider who formed America's first Company of Girl Scouts in 1912

and baths, Mrs Low having walled up part of the kitchen to make space for a bathroom. Another friend, Mrs Choate, helped her to give wonderful American tea-parties, with ice-cream and strawberries.

At this great World Camp a spectacular pageant was given by the Girl Scouts of the U.S.A., who then presented a tree to Foxlease in memory of their historic visit and asked their Founder, Mrs Low, to plant it.

The Link was kept for the entertainment of Guides and Girl Scouts of all nations, colours and creeds. Some years ago the sitting-room was refurnished by Juliette Low's British Guide friends, to commemorate the woman who had done so much for the Movement and brought Guides and Girl Scouts so close together. Over the door these simple words were carved on a plaque:

JULIETTE LOW
UNITED STATES GREAT BRITAIN

Before her death fifteen years after starting the Girl Scout Movement in America the National Board of the Girl Scouts of America sent her this telegram: *You are not only the first Girl Scout—but the best Girl Scout of them all.*

"The Birthplace", the handsome Regency mansion in Savannah where "Miss Daisy" was born, was bought by the Girl Scouts of America in 1953 after being threatened with demolition. It is now filled with mementoes of the great pioneer Guider who formed the first Company of Girl Scouts in America in 1912. Juliette Low's supreme memorial, however, is every one of the four million Girl Scouts in the U.S.A. today.

Little Blackbird

by Jennifer Maxwell-Stewart

A Guide of the 4th Banstead (St. Anne's) Company, Surrey

Sweet little blackbird,
You sit there all day
Up in the tree,
Chirping away.
Won't you come down
And sing to me?
Come right down
From your laurel tree.
I love to hear your little song;
I listen to it all day long.
No other bird like you can cry—
Please tell me, blackbird,
Please tell me why.

Search for the Thames

With Julie, Susan, Vicki, and the Editor

When I asked three Guides, Julie Cox, Susan Court and Vicki Fenley, of the 15th Cheltenham (St. Peter's, Leckhampton) Company, where the River Thames began, they all replied promptly, "At the Seven Springs."

I begged leave to differ. The fact was, I'd cunningly read the subject up beforehand and discovered that Thames Head is the real source of the Thames! The Seven Springs is on the outskirts of Cheltenham, so naturally the Cheltenham Guides tended to bestow on it the honour of being the source of Britain's premier river. Besides, lots of people believe it to be so.

We decided to settle the question by going on a tour of discovery. Let me admit right away that the Seven Springs *looks* much more like the source than Thames Head. It lies just off the Cheltenham-Cirencester road (A 435) and the Andoversford-Crickley Hill road (A 436) in a dip overhung with foliage. There is a shallow pool with stepping-stones across, and this is bounded by a high stone wall bearing the following Latin inscription:

HIC TUUS
O TAMESINE PATER
SEPTEMGEMINUS FONS
T.S.E.

I don't know who T.S.E., the chap responsible for the inscription, was, but he was obviously a worthy man and a sound Latin scholar. Quite clearly he believed that the Seven Springs was the source of the Thames, and there is added support for his belief in that on the other side of the road there is a big pool or lake formed and fed by the Seven Springs.

The Guides' confidence began to be eroded, though, as we drove on to Cirencester, for I produced literature and newspaper cuttings in which Oxford University professors made out a pretty conclusive case against the Seven Springs being the fountainhead of the Thames and insisted on giving the honour to Thames Head, near the village of Coates, just off the Cirencester-Tetbury road, A 443.

"The sign at the Seven Springs didn't actually say it was the source," admitted Susan, "so it mightn't be."

"Even professors can be wrong," hinted Vicki darkly.

"Perhaps we'll find out for sure when we see Thames Head," said Julie, very sensibly.

Just before the village of Coates, on the left-hand side of the road, we saw a signpost, which said SOURCE OF THAMES. This shook us all. The bare, unequivocal statement, SOURCE OF THAMES, was flat and final. It brooked of

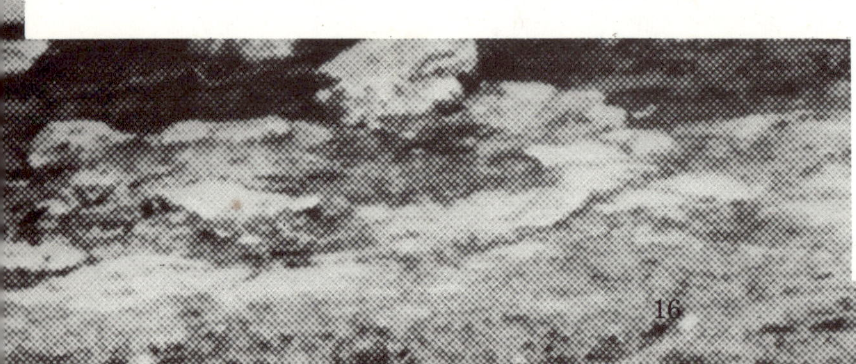

no argument. "Thames Head is the source of the Thames, and that's all there is to it," it seemed to say. "Any other place claiming to be is telling whoppers."

A walk of about a mile, on which we crossed the old, disused and overgrown Sapperton Canal, brought us to Thames Head. We knew we'd got there because of the statue of Father Thames in stone seated or reclining within a square of iron railings. Without the statue, we might have gone for miles looking for a pool or even a spring of water. For at the real, genuine, authentic, fully documented source of the Thames there isn't a drop of water—not a puddle.

This was disappointing, but Father Thames himself we all thought distinctly striking. The Guides took to him instantly.

"They might at least have put a drinking fountain here," one of the Guides remarked.

An inscription on the base of Father Thames's plinth records:

THIS STATUE WAS PLACED HERE
BY THE CONSERVATORS TO MARK
THE SOURCE OF THE RIVER
THAMES. THIS STATUE WAS
GIVEN BY H. SCOTT FREEMAN,
ESQ., CONSERVATOR.
SIR JOCELYN BRAY, D.L., J.P.
CHAIRMAN
CONSERVATORS OF THE RIVER
THAMES
1958

Sorting through my literature, the Guides informed me that the statue is supposed to have come from the site of the original Crystal Palace, London, which was burned down long before they were born.

Julie points to the signpost lettered SOURCE OF THAMES *as Vicki follows her and Susan over the stile that leads to Thames Head*

True, he's been somewhat mutilated by vandals, but he's an impressive figure in stone, much more than life-size. If he ever thinks, he must wonder who in the world put him down in a remote meadow without a drop of water to look at or drink.

"If that's so," I said, "how is it that the inscription credits H. Scott Freeman, Esq. with giving it?"

The Guides seemed to think the question irrelevant.

Well, wherever he came from, Father Thames was put there, at the fountainhead of one of the world's great rivers.

He has not, however, been allowed to rest there, for only a few months after we paid him a visit the Thames Water Authority decided he'd taken enough from airgun pellets and other

Vicki contemplates the statue of Father Thames, battered by wind, rain and vandals, as he reclines in his iron cage with never a drop of water to look at or drink

missiles and moved him to Swindon for repair and restoration and then to a, one hopes, permanent resting-place in the garden of a lock-keeper's cottage at Lechlade. There at last he's able to look upon water! At the actual source a two-ton block of Cornish granite, suitably inscribed, has been placed. —R.M.

The block of Cornish granite that has replaced the statue of Father Thames at Thames Head

Colour slides by ***Robert Moss***

it's a good idea -

says Rosemary B. Christopher

Personal Designs

It's easy and it's fun to decorate plain nylon scarves, blouses or babies' dresses, or cotton tee shirts, with your own personal and colourful designs. You can draw your designs with a black-ink pen or use an embroidery transfer on the nylon articles. For the cotton tee shirts you can iron on a transfer as used for embroidery or pin the material flat to a board and trace the design on to it. If you are using nylon put the transfer or drawing under the material so that the pattern shows through.

Colour in the pattern on either material, using ordinary wax crayons, not coloured pencils. Remove the drawing when it is all coloured. Place the material on a sheet of blotting-paper, and cover with another piece of blotting-paper. Press with an iron that is just warm. The blotting-paper absorbs the wax, leaving the design neatly and indelibly printed on the material.

When the garment needs washing, use warm soapy (not detergent) water.

Pin Pusher

When you have the job of putting up several notices on a notice-board, or decorating a stage or bazaar stall, don't make your fingers sore pushing in all those drawing-pins, or risk breaking finger-nails. Keep a thimble in your pocket, and wear it to push the drawing-pins in with.

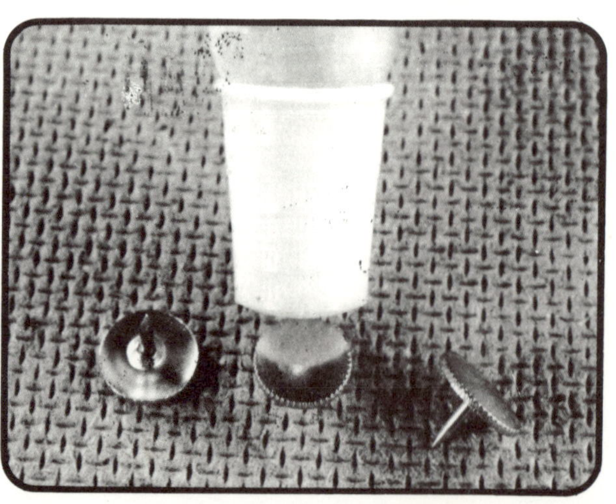

Belt-Hanger

Use a wooden coathanger to keep all your belts in good order. Simply screw some small hooks (as used with curtain wires) along one side of the coat-hanger. An ordinary hanger will hold about a dozen belts, and it makes keeping your room tidy much easier. It also saves precious time when you're looking for a particular belt. Such a hanger would make a good useful Christmas present for aunties or elder sisters.

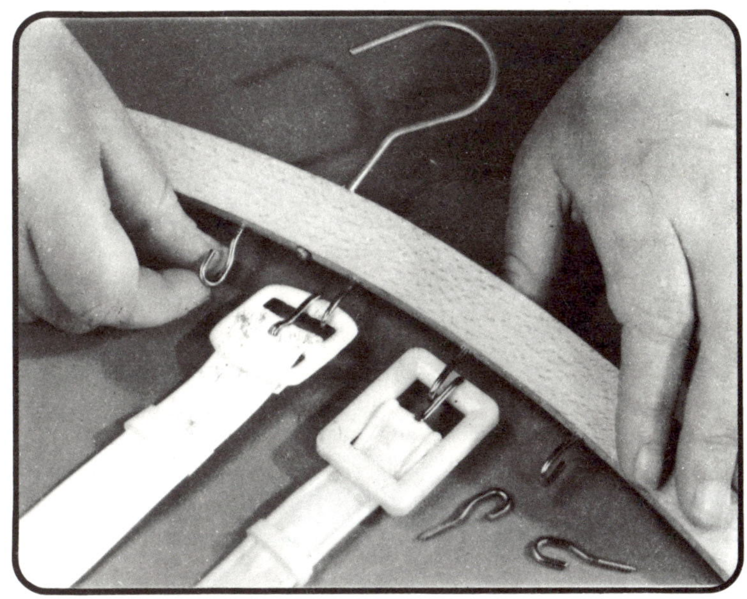

CAMP

DODSworth.

"They followed me home"

Colour slide by ***Miss E. Paterson***

Colour slides by ***Mrs J. Fisher***

WHAT'S COOKING?

A Patrol Leader at Netherurd cooking for the Backwoodsman badge

The proof of the cooking is in the eating

These Guides of the 24th York Dinghouses Company believe in cooking by modern methods

HOME AND AWAY

New Zealand Guides outside their headquarters which is fronted by a Maori post of native wood intricately carved

Canadian Guides of the 68th Toronto Company proudly wear the Blue Cords they have just been awarded

Guides of the 1st Whitley Bay Company distribute programmes at the Northumberland Horse Show

Out with a

Last spring, five Guides from the 1st Whittle-le-Woods and Clayton Company, near Chorley, Lancashire, accompanied me on a project – photographing wild life, specifically a lapwing.

The lapwing was occupying a rushy field not far from my home. The nesting-field was close to a farmhouse, and the farmer had kindly agreed to keep a watch on the nest and the bird.

Our first job was to locate the actual nest. This was not as easy as searching for a nest in a hedge. The field is a large one of several acres, so I did what I normally do when searching for the nests of ground nesters – pinpoint the female with binoculars by peering through the hedge, then make a dash into the field, marking with my eye the place where the bird rises. Even by doing this it took the Guides and me about fifteen minutes to locate the site. The nest was open to the sky, but the eggs are so marked as to make it difficult to spot them in the shallow hollow that is the nest.

The eggs of the lapwing are heavily spotted with dark-brown and black. They are large for the size of the bird. They are pointed at one end and arranged in a circle with their points facing inwards; otherwise the bird would not be able to cover them. The normal clutch is four eggs.

We erected the photographic hide – made of light canvas – about fourteen metres from the nest. If the hide had been placed in the final photographic position first, the bird would have forsaken her eggs, and a very black mark is awarded to any photographer who allows this to happen.

With the hide firmly secured and guyed we packed up, but before finally departing made sure that the bird and its mate had accepted the hide that had suddenly "grown" in the middle of the field. Through binoculars we watched the female sweep across the field on her broad wings and land some five metres from her nest, then walk the rest of the way.

The next morning we moved the hide two metres towards the nest, and secured it as before. This move was made several times until the hide was about seven metres from the nest. After two days in this position we could attempt photography.

The author, wildlife photographer ***Michael P. Edwards****, sets out on a photographic session*

Wildlife Photographer

Michael P. Edwards

The weather was ideal—sunny and still. The camera equipment was put together before we entered the field, so avoiding keeping the bird off its nest unnecessarily. The camera I use is a 35mm, very popular with wildlife photographers. I told the Guides how the camera worked and about the various lenses. The lens I was going to use was a 400mm telephoto, which enables

Michael Edwards lines up a subject —and prepares to wait. Patience is a quality a wildlife photographer must cultivate to be successful

The Guides on their way to the photographic location

The photographic hide is like a small tent, and is easy to erect

It is easy to see from this photograph how the bird acquired its other name of green plover

close-up pictures to be taken from a distance. As lapwings are rather nervous, too close an approach makes them restless, and this becomes evident in pictures taken by photographers who have not realised this.

The Guides accompanied me to the hide and fastened the flaps, then hid in one of the outbuildings at the field's edge. Within a few minutes a dark shadow crossed the hide, and the female alighted not far from the eggs. When viewed from a distance, the lapwing appears to be black-and-white, but close up, with the sun on its back, it is seen to be a very beautiful bird, as you can see yourselves from the pictures we took.

When the session was concluded, I pushed a white handkerchief through a hole in the back of the hide. This was a sign to the Guides to relieve me. This last part is vital. If I were to appear suddenly from the hide the bird would receive such a fright that it might cause her to abandon the nest. The Guides approaching slowly from a distance gave the bird scope for leaving her eggs at leisure.

You can judge for yourselves from the pictures how successful this project was. It was certainly enjoyable for the Guides—and for me.

Looking through powerful binoculars, the Guides satisfy themselves that the birds are not disturbed by the hide that has "grown up" in the middle of the field

The lapwing's eggs in the nest. The markings make them difficult to detect

Guides prepare a meal at camp on the island of Maraki. Their uniform is a short-sleeved blue dress with a scarf of Company colour and a blue headband with badge

Guides of a

by Elizabeth Paterson

Let us go half way round the world, right to the other side, to a remote group of palm-covered islands, just west of the International Dateline. The islands are flat and low, no point being higher than 12 feet above sea-level, and each one is surrounded by a coral reef.

Where are we? We are on the Gilbert and Ellice Islands Colony, where the sun shines every day and it never gets cold. There are twenty-six main inhabited islands. Most islanders live in neat, pleasant villages by the sea, in cool thatched houses. Water comes from a well, and the toilet is a little house built over the sea! Cooking is done outside on an open fire, and paraffin lamps are lit when it gets dark.

The islands are scattered over an area larger than Australia, and transport between the islands is a great problem, many of the islands being visited by a ship only every two or three months. Several of the larger islands have a truck or a tractor; most of the islands have several motor-bikes, and all of them have lots of bicycles. However, the most common form of transport is by canoe, as the Gilbert and Ellice islanders are great sailors and excellent navigators. Canoes are all built with outriggers and have one large triangular sail.

Guide meetings usually take place in the afternoon, in the cool *maneaba*, the meeting-house of the village, or in a shady clearing among the coconut trees. The Guides may belong to the Frangipani, Hibiscus or Bougainvilia Patrol and come to the meeting with their sweet-smelling emblem in their hair! A short-sleeved blue

The Guide Guider lays the table inside her matting-and-thatch home on the island of Makin

Tropical Island

Photos and colour slides by ***Miss E. Paterson***

dress, rather like a camp overall, is the uniform, with a coloured scarf, a blue material belt and a hat-band. There is no need to wear socks or shoes, nor a pull-over. Every Guide has long, black, shiny hair, which may be tied back or plaited or caught up in a knot on the top of her head; it is never, never untidy!

The Guides in the Gilbert and Ellice follow a special Pacific programme. The Promise, Law and Motto are just the same as in this country, and the Guides play many of the games that you do, and take part in the same type of activities. When they learn first-aid, they have to be able to deal with poison from insects or fish, or they might help in the village by cleaning out the well, or make string to sell for some good cause. If they are going for a hike, they will usually set off early in the morning, before it gets too hot, and will carry some fish, or perhaps some bread or babai (a root vegetable) and a piece of coconut to chew. When the Guides get thirsty one of them will climb a coconut-tree and throw down some young nuts full of fresh, cool milk.

Gilbert and Ellice people are very clever with their hands and make many beautiful things. The Guides and Scouts are encouraged to learn these traditional skills. The Guides weave fine mats, baskets of all shapes and sizes, hats to keep the sun off, and very lovely fans to help keep cool. Crochet and embroidery are also very popular. Scouts are skilled in making fishing traps, furniture for the house, and small model canoes. Before anyone leaves an island he or she is

An early-morning wash Gilbert and Ellice style

given as a good-luck token a necklace made of small cowrie shells. The Guides will collect the shells, make a tiny hole in each and thread them on to nylon fishing line.

Camping is very popular. Sometimes the Guides will go to another village and stay in the *maneaba*, or go by canoe to a small island across the lagoon, where they will sleep in shelters put up by the men who come to cut copra once or twice a year from the main island. If the Guides go to a completely deserted place, they will take some Scouts with them to help build the shelters. On Tarawa, the capital, the Guides lease a small island called Guide Island, and when they go to camp here they use tents. The Guides do not take very much food with them to camp, as they will fish in the shallow water with a net and perhaps hunt for small octopus by torchlight in the evening; or just at dusk they will go and catch crabs as these leave their holes to search for food. Coconuts, breadfruit and bananas will also be collected, and they will bake their own bread, pancakes and doughnuts.

There is no television on the island and only about twenty-four hours of radio a week! Tarawa is the only island with

Patrol Leaders in council, with the mameaba (meeting-house) in the background

A dance in traditional grass skirts

a cinema. Everyone lives by the sea. The water is always warm and there are nice sandy beaches to play on. Volley ball is one of the most popular games that the people play, although they play lots of local games as well. In the evening there is traditional dancing in grass skirts, or modern dancing at an "island night". Singing is enjoyed and there are lots of choirs. An old man may tell stories of long ago, or a sailor tell of his recent voyage to America, Hong Kong or Japan.

At festival times like Easter, Christmas and the Queen's Birthday, competitions are held between the villages. All the people on an island will gather at one place and hold canoe races and volley-ball games; the choirs and dancing teams will also compete. In the evenings there will be great feasting, with everyone in their best clothes. To eat, there will be a whole pig cooked in an underground oven, and several huge tuna fish cooked in the same way. Raw fish in coconut milk will also be served, as this is a speciality of the islands. The women will produce lots of exciting dishes only made on special occasions.

The old men of the village will make some speeches, and so will any stranger at the feast; after which he will not be a stranger but a welcome guest.

The Water Patrol. Guides on the islands seldom wear shoes or sandals

Morse Code Crossword

by Daphne Pilcher

How well do you know the Morse Code? This novel crossword puzzle will help to impress it on your mind. The numbers shown (**a** for **across** and **d** for **down**) with dots and dashes make up initials—as, for example, 1a and 3a spell out BP, the initials of the Founder of Scouts and Guides. Read the Morse in the other squares in the sequence shown below without, if possible, looking at the code in the *Guide Handbook.*

1a and **3a**
12a, 13a, 2d
18d, 20a, 1d
16d and **6a**
7d, 23a and **11a**
21a, 10d and **8a**
14d and **5a**
4d and **19d**
9 and **22a**
17a and **15**

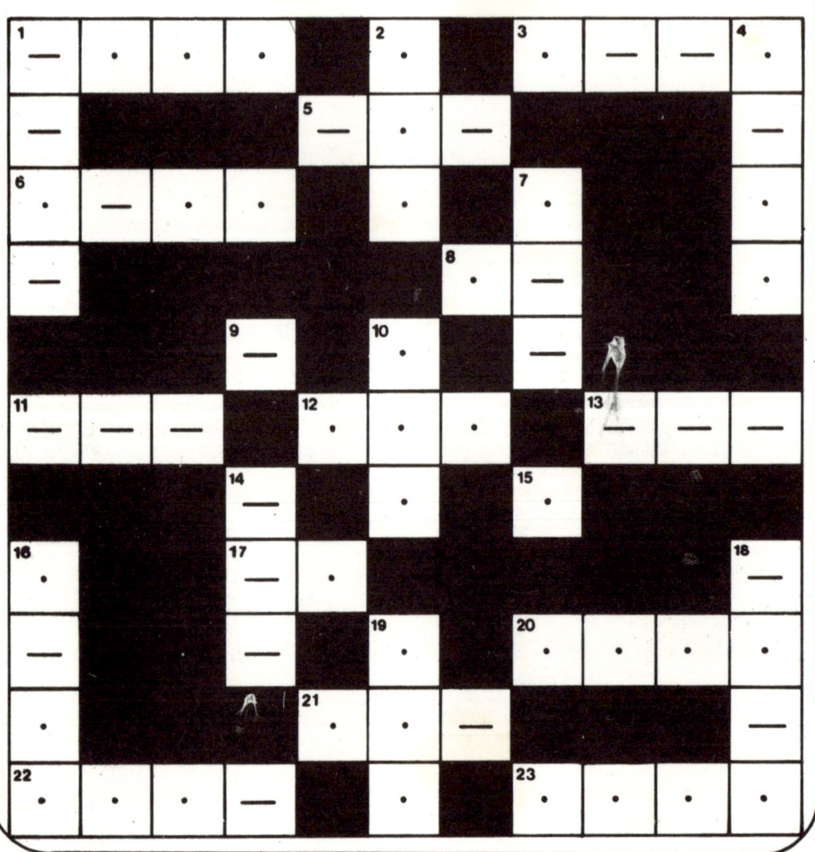

TV Treasure Hunt

Here is a game you'll be able to play on a wet day. It's a variation of the usual kind of treasure hunt, with the added advantage that it requires little preparation.

Announce the name of a well-known TV "star"—preferably one with a fairly short name, for example: Forsyth, Andrews, Crowther, or Howerd.

This "star" must then be brought into the party by collecting a number of articles which have initial letters that make his name.

Thus, if Howerd is chosen, the treasure-hunter might collect a hat, an orange, a woggle, an envelope, a rope, and a dixie. The first player to succeed is the winner. —S.M.B.

"Mind you, it's going to be crowded in our tent"

Sand Castles for the Party

by M. I. Eckhardt

To make jelly or blancmange sand castles you will need a packet of jelly or blancmange, empty mousse containers, an icing set, cream, jelly tots, a cocktail stick, marzipan.

Make up the jelly according to the instructions on the packet. Rinse the mousse containers in cold water before pouring the jelly in. Leave in a cool place to set. When set, empty out into dishes. Pipe cream round the jelly "castle", placing jelly tots or something similar on it at intervals to represent shells. A squirt of cream on top of the "castle" with a marzipan flag on a cocktail stick in it completes an attractive party dish for children.

The Enchanted Island

By Karen Barned

A Guide of the 1st Joyden's Wood Company, Kent

Where the winding river widens,
Where the trees are far apart,
Where the children play so gaily,
Where the horses have no cart,
Where the hills are green and scattered,
Where the stars do gleam at night,
Where nearly everything is sparkling,
Where the moon is big and bright,
Where all the animals are grazing,
Skipping, jumping in the air,
Where the people lie and slumber,
Living things are everywhere.
Who is he that lies and wonders
Where this lovely place can be,
Where the houses have no water,
Get their water from the sea?

Treacle scones are delicious—if you can get a bite at them

HALLOWE'EN PARTY

Colour slides by Miss E. M. Leishman

Guides of the 2nd Wick (Caithness, Scotland) Company make turnip lanterns for Hallowe'en

FIND THE FLOWERS

by A. L. Blowers

Can you find these flowers in the garden? Some grow wild as well.

1. Coloured percussion instrument
2. Remember me
3. An important virtue
4. Will burn your hand
5. Waits for no man
6. Ingredient in soup
7. Moses saw this
8. A good habit
9. A city percussion object
10. Part of the eye
11. Part of a watering-can

COIN QUIZ

Here are the emblems on the six coins in use in Great Britain.

Can you say without looking at the coins in your purse or your money-box which emblems belong to which coin?

The coins are ½p, 1p, 2p, 5p, 10p, and 50p.

BIRD CROSSWORD

ACROSS

5. What Scout Job Week used to be called
8. Much favoured at camp
9. Makes the wheels go round
11. For tea at camp in quantity
14. Male
15. Thread of a rope
16. Guides like camping here
17. More than a pot
18. Mind it's a good one
19. Found in a window
20. For crumble or pie
21. Neither hot nor cold
22. Same word as 11 but spelt differently
23. A sealed one with food is a good stand-by
24. Jellies should
25. First number

DOWN

1. For the camp-fire
2. Used to be
3. See wild animals here
4. Often by the hearth
5. Not good
6. Place to sleep
7. Don't run up one
8. Campers look for these
10. Self
11. You and me
12. Short sleep
13. Nothing
14. Male
15. Thread of a rope
17. More than a pot
18. Mind it's a good one
19. Found in a window
21. You'll find it camping on a hill-top
23. Towards

The Wheel~Chair Guide

by Jane Walton

Lisa wasn't cruel or unkind, but she was ambitious for her Patrol. They were a very good Patrol. There was recognition in the Company that the Robins were the elite Patrol of the Company. They had wide interests, they were all keen on different aspects of Guiding, and Lisa was a good Leader.

Then Kate arrived.

Kate came from Brennan's, the spastics' home. She was in a wheel-chair—and she was put into the Robin Patrol.

Lisa set her face into a smile and endured a dreadful first meeting. Kate failed from sheer nervousness in everything she did. Her neat hands fumbled with the wheels of her chair, and she thumped and crashed all over the hall as she struggled to join in the activities of the Patrol. Others tried to help, but Lisa harried them impatiently.

Gradually, over the weeks, the Robin Patrol lost most of its glamour, but it gained too. The rest of the Company watched with sympathy and approval as the Robins learned to accept defeats with grace and humour. The old idea of an elite melted away, and other Patrols were able to shine with their particular lights for a while. The whole Company grew more comfortable.

Kate flourished, but Lisa didn't.

"It isn't fair." she muttered to

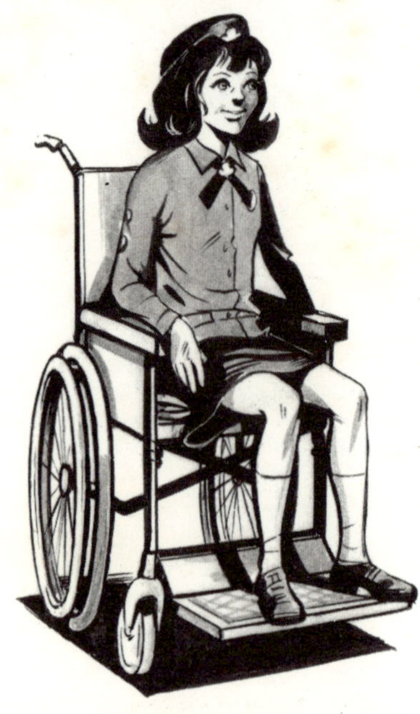

Jan, her best friend. "Why should we have to have Kate all the time?"

Lisa couldn't forgive Kate for her slowness or her clumsy attempts to join in some of the Patrol's activities. Even when the Patrol benefited from the use of Kate's chair—she could carry so much more at a time than anyone else—Lisa didn't relent.

Jan knew better than to argue with Lisa, but she tried to soothe her.

"Never mind," she said. "It's camp next month, and Kate isn't coming; I heard her tell Miss Lake."

Lisa sighed with relief. "Then we'll stand a chance of winning some of the camp competitions."

She smiled and forgot the aggravations of the past as she anticipated the triumphs to come. She was even more pleased when Kate missed the last two meetings before camp and pressed the Robins to make their preparations perfect.

"Calm down, Lisa," begged Jan, as she sewed on buttons, but Lisa was excited and thankful.

"Camp without Kate!" she sighed. "How great!"

The Guides set off in a large coach to go to the woods where their autumn camp was usually held. It was a good place. The surrounding trees gave an illusion of distance, but the village was conveniently near. Its people knew and liked the Guides. It pleased them to see the girls' activities, and they were used to seeing Guides racing down the broad rides of the woodland or climbing up the paths of the higher thickets.

The camp lasted a week. Right up to Friday all went well, especially for the Robin Patrol. The Robins were star turns at cooking and woodcraft, and they conceived and acted an hilarious sketch that kept the whole camp convulsed at the Friday concert.

On Saturday, the last afternoon was to be spent tracking and treasure-hunting, and the Robins looked forward to it eagerly.

Then Kate arrived.

Her brother was with her, in

full Scout uniform. He helped Kate out of a car and settled her in a wheel-chair. He came into camp pushing her along at a brisk pace.

"Miss Lake?" he inquired. "I'm down on a visit to our Kate, and when she told me that she was missing camp I volunteered to be her legs!"

"You're most welcome," smiled the Guider. "Kate, we've missed you, but I thought you were in hospital."

"I was." Kate exhibited a bandaged but stiffly straight leg. "I've had my leg done, Miss Lake. I'll soon be able to walk—with sticks," she added ruefully.

The Guides crowded round to welcome Kate—except Lisa, who was quietly furious.

"This is wonderful news," said the Guider. "What about this afternoon? We are just off tracking and treasure-hunting."

"No problem," grinned Jack, as he looked down at a wistful Kate. "I can tote Kate anywhere—if the rules allow for that."

"Of course you can come!" said Miss Lake, and all the Guides signified their approval—except Lisa.

The briefing for the afternoon was exact. "The trail ends somewhere in Deep Copse," Miss Lake told them, "but it's a very tricky one to follow and I shall check on every sign. Now listen carefully. If you are not in Deep Copse by five o'clock, turn back. I don't want any of you in these woods at dusk. Turn back at five wherever you are. Now, don't miss one sign. They are all numbered, so you must find them in order."

One or two of the girls shivered a little with enjoyable fear, for Miss Lake was a great storyteller and the shadows behind the campfire circle gave the girls a feeling of tension when a Deep Copse story was in the evening repertoire.

The Guider repeated, "No one in Deep Copse after dusk," and the hunt was on.

Kate was so frail that Jack could easily lift her over any obstacle. The wheel-chair was very light, and even Jan, who had appointed herself helper, was able to lift it easily. Kate's progress was certainly no hindrance to the Patrol. Indeed, she proved quite a help, for, as Jack pushed vigorously and Kate was bowled along quickly, she spotted the tracking signs first.

"It's because I don't have to concentrate on anything else," she explained shyly.

Kate spotted the tracking signs first.

Even Lisa reluctantly agreed she deserved congratulations on her sign-spotting.

The Robin Patrol were far ahead of any other when, as the afternoon sun faded, they found themselves in a rocky dell hugged closely by trees.

Kate's laugh rang out as she was again first to spot a sign. In one of the trees sat an "owl", a felt one that looked realistic among the leaves. In the "owl's" beak was a folded note. Lisa scrambled up for it. She handed the "owl" to Sally, the Patrol's best runner.

"Wait!" she cried as she read the note. "Look!" She showed the girls a map on which was marked a short cut home.

The path shown was obviously short and steep. Sally was soon away, with the others following almost as quickly. Lisa saw Jan turn to Jack with an enquiry in her eyes.

"No, Jan," said Lisa. "It's my turn."

Jan nodded and ran off after the others. She smiled, thankful that at last Lisa's prejudice against the wheel-chair Guide was dying.

Lisa turned to Kate, but the frail girl shook her head.

"No, Lisa! Thank you very much, but not even Jack could manoeuvre me through that track. You go ahead. We'll take the long way back."

Jack joined in. "Go on, Lisa. You ought to catch up the others. It's getting very near to Miss Lake's dusk."

Lisa nodded. "You gained us the prize," she acknowledged. She turned to plunge down the path—and fell. She cried out in sudden pain. Kate could see that her face had drained white. Kate backed away to let Jack get by.

He bent down to lift Lisa—and couldn't.

Jack was gentle, but Lisa was clearly in severe pain.

"No bones broken," he reassured his sister.

Lisa tried to take command of the situation.

"Jack," she begged, "get Kate away. You can send someone back for me," but she shivered with uncontrollable apprehension.

"Stop being so brave," said Jack bluntly. "You're the patient now. I think I can carry you to the edge of Deep Copse. It's only a minute from there to the first cottage. I'll take you first and come back for Kate."

He bent down to lift Lisa—and couldn't.

"Kate and I are the same age but not the same weight," Lisa whispered faintly through set teeth.

For the first time Jack looked worried.

A thud behind them startled them both. Kate had propelled herself out of her chair. She lay in an untidy heap on the grass, and one skinny hand was pushing the chair nearer to Lisa.

"Use this, Jack," she puffed breathlessly. "I'll stay here—but hurry!"

"It's getting dusk. You can't stay alone," Lisa objected.

Jack grinned, "You don't know our Kate." His voice glowed with pride. "She can face anything, even ghosties."

He went to her to make her more comfortable, but she waved him off. "Get going, Jack," she said, almost crossly.

"I'll be quick," he promised. He cast an anxious look at her thin, white face.

Kate managed a small smile as he trundled Lisa off in the wheel-chair.

He wasn't quick. What nad been easy with lightweight Kate was hard with the much heavier Lisa. The chair creaked and groaned. Then the owners of the first house were out, so Jack had to push on down the village street to another cottage. Explanations were lengthy, and it was over an hour before he and the village nurse got back with torches and blankets to find Kate cold, semi-conscious and, worst of all, with her leg in its bandages thrust forward at an awkward angle.

"We'd better get her to hospital," said the nurse.

In the hospital a doctor looked at Jack's strained face and said, "Don't worry too much, young man. I'll guarantee your sister won't. She's a lot tougher than she looks."

He was right about Kate, whose first inquiry was whether Lisa was all right.

"She is," replied the doctor, "thanks to your wheel-chair. If she'd tried to walk on that leg she might have done herself bad damage. Your Guider, Miss Lake, has brought her in here for the night. She'll be better here than in camp."

Kate wanted him to tell her more, but at that moment the door opened and Lisa came in—in a wheel-chair.

"Now I'll learn," she told Kate, grinning.

Miss Lake, coming up the corridor outside, wondered why there was so much laughter coming from the other side of the door.

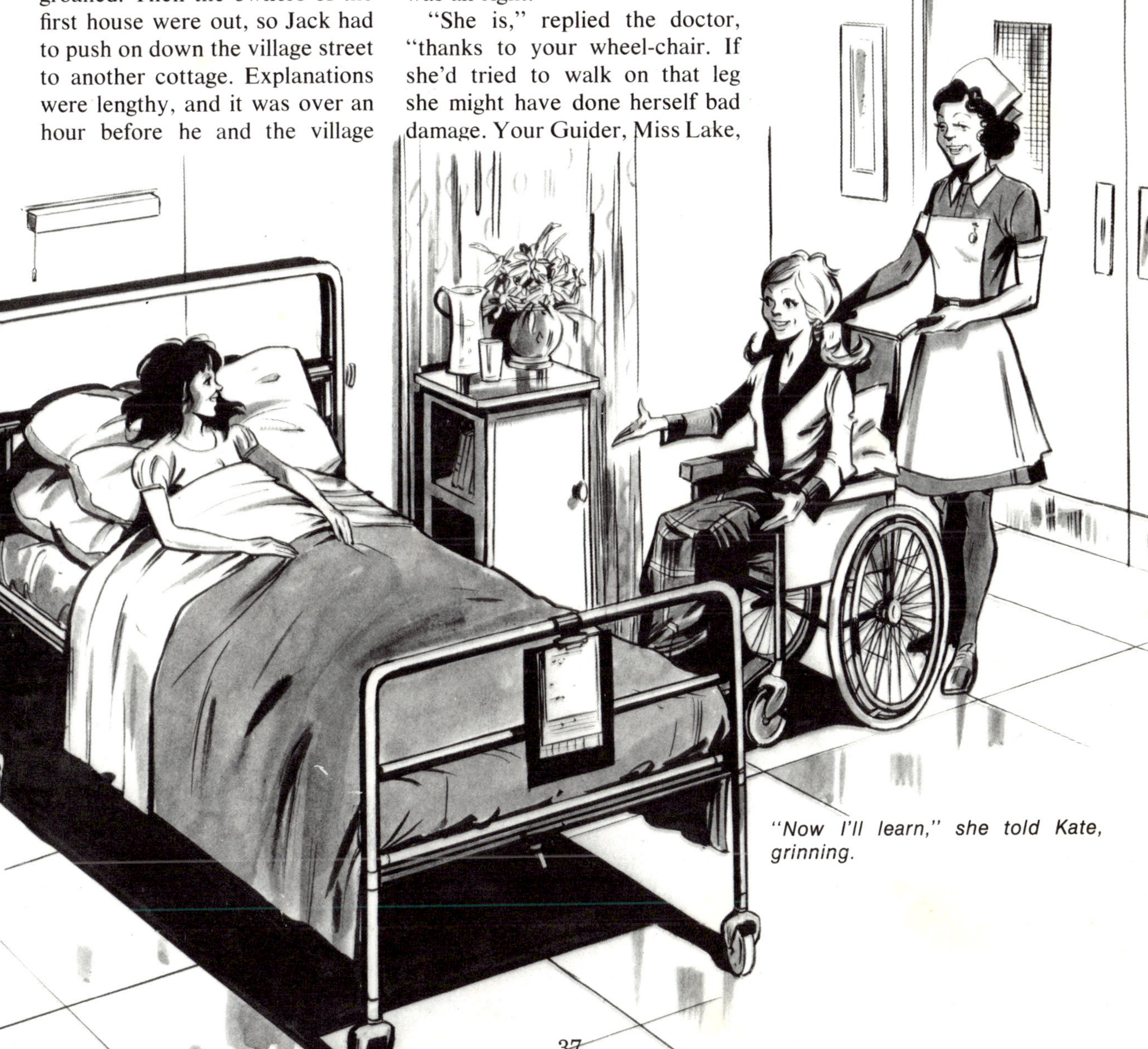

"Now I'll learn," she told Kate, grinning.

Useful Things to Make for Patrol Corner, Camp and Home

by Celeste Zapotoczny

WHATNOT BOX. Here's a sure seller for the Guide stall and an unusual gift for a deserving father's desk or bureau.

Materials required are:

Two small matchboxes

Two wing-type paper-fasteners

Scraps of wallpaper, wrapping paper or self-adhesive paper

Clear shellac.

First glue two matchboxes on top of each other. Wrap the sides, top and back of this "cabinet" in a piece of wallpaper, wrapping paper or self-adhesive paper.

Now insert a push-through paper-fastener into the centre of each drawer for ease in opening.

A light coat of clear shellac will preserve the finish of the paper wrap. If self-adhesive paper is used, shellac is not necessary.

This "whatnot" makes an ideal container for paper-clips, rubber bands, drawing-pins, and other small items that often get misplaced.

BUTTON BOX. A button box is a commonplace thing, but here's a way to make it look attractive. You will need:

Small coffee can with lid

Gold paint

Gold glitter

Varied shapes of macaroni

Small dried beans or peas (optional).

Glue various shapes of macaroni and small dried beans or peas in a pretty design on the coffee-can lid. When dry, lightly spray or brush gold paint on lid and can. After the base-coat has dried, paint again. Do not allow this coat to dry completely. While it is still "tacky" sprinkle gold glitter all over lid and can.

Now you have a button box that mothers will appreciate as a gift or that can be sold at a sale-of-work.

PENCIL-HOLDER. To make an attractive pencil-holder for Dad's desk or Mum's kitchen or for the Guide stall at a fund-raising sale, you will need:

One tin can

Paint (any colour)

Scraps of coloured felt material.

Remove labels from can. Paint it the colour of your choice. Add a second coat when the base coat is dry. When the second coat has dried completely (preferably overnight) glue various designs and shapes cut from brightly coloured felt to the can.

FANCY LIGHT-SWITCH PLATES. Have you ever thought of adding a decorative touch to the light-switch plates in your bedroom? It's quite easily done. All you need are small beads or tiny seashells.

Carefully unscrew the light-switch plate from the wall. Glue small beads or tiny coloured seashells on the border of the plate. Let them dry overnight. When dry, replace the plate on the wall.

This dainty touch will add something to the decor of your room.

Sit-upons are useful things to have at camp or on a hike. They're easy to make. You'll need the following:

Several old newspapers

Oilcloth (two pieces, 16″ × 16″: 40·5 × 40·5 cm)

Coloured rug yarn

Large darning needle.

Fold whole sheets of newspaper lengthwise into 3″-wide (7·5 cm) strips. Lay five of these strips vertically close together. Next, weave five other strips through these horizontally. Keep smoothing, so that the mat will be flat.

Cut two pieces of oilcloth, 16″ × 16″. Punch holes approximately 1″ (2·5 cm) apart along the entire border of both pieces. Place the woven newspaper mat carefully between the two pieces of oilcloth and stitch through holes with brightly coloured rug yarn.

These sit-upons are waterproof and absorb cold and damp well and are ideal for when you need to sit on the ground.

CUPBOARD FRESHENER. This makes an acceptable gift and is easily made from the following materials:

One medium-size orange

One packet of whole cloves

Nylon net cut into 8″ (20 cm) squares

Ribbon.

Cover a medium-size orange with whole cloves by securely pushing each clove into the skin and pulpy part of the orange.

When the orange is completely covered, wrap with a square of coloured nylon and tie with a length of ribbon.

This cupboard freshener will retain its fragrance for well over a year. It can be hung on to a wardrobe rod or over a coat-hanger.

RECIPE FILE. A handy recipe file can be made from the following materials:

One packet of index cards, lined, 5″ × 3″ (12·5 cm × 7·5 cm)

One large ring-binder.

Get each member of your Patrol to bring in one of her mother's favourite recipes. Each Patrol member should make a copy of her recipe on the index-cards for all the other members of the Patrol.

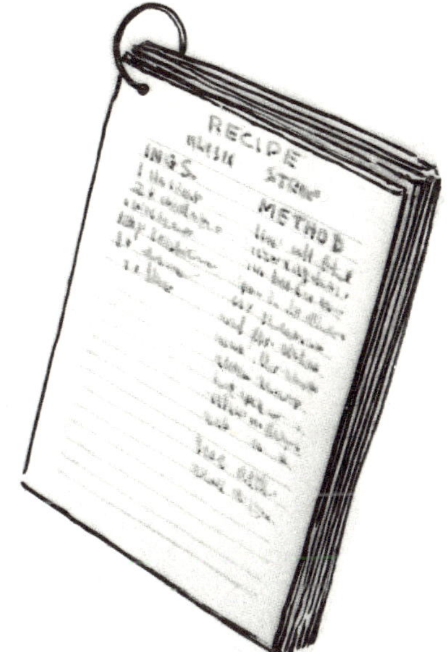

At the upper left-hand corner of the index-cards, including the cards still blank, punch a hole and fasten all the cards together with the large ring-binder.

These recipes will be very handy for mothers, as they can be hung in the kitchen and be added to as further recipes are tried out. As all the recipes are fastened together, reference becomes very easy and the cards won't get misplaced or damaged.

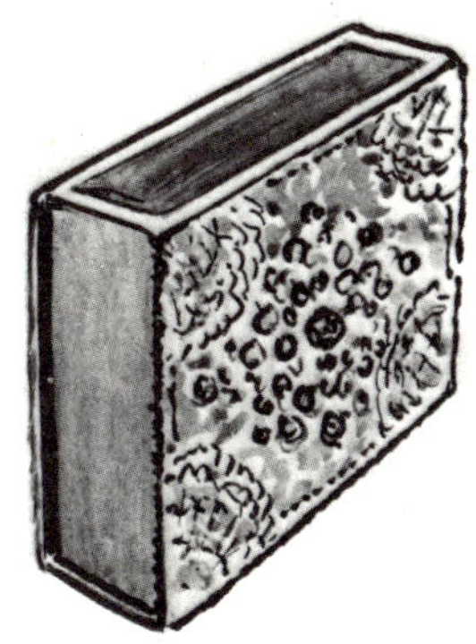

JEWELLED MATCHBOXES. These sound very grand, but are in fact ordinary matchboxes dressed up attractively with odds and ends. For decoration you will need:

Scraps of different fabrics

Bits of ric-rac or lace

Sequins, small beads, bits of discarded jewellery.

Begin by glueing a piece of fabric on the top of a matchbox, leaving the sides uncovered. Next, decorate the top to your own taste with sequins, small beads, ric-rac, lace or bits of discarded jewellery.

Large matchboxes can also be decorated in this way. They make nice little gifts that will sell readily on a Guide stall.

Weather recording and forecasting can be fun and can lead to the Weatherman badge, which can help you

The Wea

Allison's job is to record the wind direction. She has found a convenient weathervane on the local riding-school and checks it daily

Family holiday transparencies often show good cloud formations. Dawn, the Patrol Leader, and Anne, her Second, have borrowed a number of slides from members of their Patrol and are identifying the clouds with the aid of a weather book

Each day Janet notes the type of cloud and how much of the sky is covered at different times (five-tenths or nine-tenths covered, for example)

qualify for the Woodcraft emblem and the Queen's Guide badge. Here is how one Patrol tackle a weather project.

hergirls

▲ The P.L. assigns a "weather job" to each Guide. Anne gives a slide show for the Patrol, demonstrating the different types of clouds

▲ Carol empties the contents, if any, into the special measuring cylinder to measure the rainfall in inches

At exactly the same time each afternoon, Carol checks how much rain has fallen in the past 24 hours. The rain-gauge has a container 30.5cm (12") high, to stop water splashing up from the ground, a funnel 12.7cm (5") diameter, and a collecting bottle ▼

◀ As soon as she gets up each morning, Loren checks the previous night's lowest temperature with a minimum/maximum thermometer. Late in the afternoon she will check the day's highest temperature. She is re-setting the thermometer with the aid of a magnet

▲ At a weekly Patrol meeting, Andrea (second from the left), who is the Patrol weather-recorder, collects all the Guides' reports and enters them in the Patrol weather-log

'tten and photographed by **A. A. Reeve**

PRUNELLA'S GOOD TURN

by M. J. Riley

ANYWAY, I GOT YOUR HANDBAG BACK FOR YOU!

YOU MUST COME WITH ME TO MY COTTAGE AND DRY YOURSELF.

GOSH, I SHOULDN'T WANT TO STAY IN GUIDES IF I HAD TO DRESS LIKE THIS! I HOPE MY UNIFORM DRIES QUICKLY. I'M TOO LATE FOR THE MEETING NOW.

TAKE YOUR WET THINGS OFF AND PUT THIS OLD UNIFORM ON. IT WAS MY GUIDER UNIFORM OVER FIFTY YEARS AGO. I JOINED THE GIRL GUIDE MOVEMENT IN ITS EARLIEST DAYS. YOU CAN WEAR THE UNIFORM WHILE YOUR OWN DRIES ON THE LINE.

FANCY YOU BEING A GUIDER ONCE, MRS BROWN!

I'LL HELP MESELF TO THEM THINGS WHEN THE OLE DEAR'S GONE IN. I'LL GET A FEW BITS O' SILVER FOR 'EM.
THE SUN WILL SOON DRY THESE OUT.

I'M NO GIRL GUIDE – THIS IS ME **BAD** TURN FOR THE DAY!

SOMETHING TERRIBLE HAS HAPPENED YOUR UNIFORM HAS GONE. SOMEONE MUST HAVE STOLEN IT FROM THE LINE.
OH, NO!

I SHALL TELL THE POLICE ABOUT THE THEFT, AND I HOPE THEY'LL GET YOUR UNIFORM BACK, PRUNELLA.
IF I'VE GOT TO GO HOME IN THIS ANTIQUITY I ONLY HOPE I DON'T MEET ANYBODY I KNOW.

WHAT'S THE BAND FOR, I WONDER? GOSH, I HOPE NO GUIDES ARE FOLLOWING AND SEE ME!

HOSPITAL FLAG DAY
HEAVENS, THERE'S THREE OF MY OWN PATROL! JUST MY LUCK TO RUN INTO THEM COMING FROM THE GUIDE MEETING! I KNOW! I'LL JOIN IN THE CROWD BEHIND THE BAND AND HOPE THEY WON'T SPOT ME.

JUDGES

WE ARE AWARDING THE FIRST PRIZE TO THE YOUNG LADY WEARING THE OLD-STYLE UNIFORM OF A GIRL GUIDE LEADER. I REMEMBER SO WELL MY MOTHER WEARING A UNIFORM LIKE THAT. WE ALL AGREE THAT THIS IS THE MOST NOVEL AND INTERESTING FANCY DRESS IN THE PARADE.
TEAS
YOU-YOU DON'T MEAN *ME?*

I HAVE PLEASURE IN HANDLING YOU A CHEQUE FOR TEN POUNDS. CONGRATULATIONS!
TH-TH-THANK YOU, SIR!

WHATEVER HAVE YOU GOT YOURSELF UP IN NOW, PRUNELLA? WHERE'S YOUR GUIDE UNIFORM? YOU LOOK LIKE-LIKE SOME-THING OUT OF THE PAST.
OUT OF THE PAST IS JUST WHAT I'M SUPPOSED TO BE, MUM. NEVER MIND ABOUT THE UNIFORM I'VE JUST WON TEN POUNDS TO BUY MYSELF A NEW ONE.

Guides of the 7th Enfield, Middlesex, stack away the washing-up on the "crockery tree"

Photos by **A. A. Reeve**

One of them refreshes herself with a good wash after collecting wood

CAMP ACTIVITIES

Guides of the 31st Portsmouth Company put the cabbage on to boil

31st Portsmouth Guides get busy in and out of their tent

Photos by **Miss W. J. Beer**

£100 PRIZE COMPETITION

Win the Double Prize of a Bike for Yourself and £50 for Your Company

Choose the stories, articles, puzzles, etc. that you specially like in the *Girl Guide Annual* and you could win a handsome new bike plus £50 for your Company!

Every Guide, regardless of age, has an equal chance of winning.

Simply pick out what you think is the best and next-best contribution in the groups listed and write the letter of your choice in the space given on the entry form.

The Editor has already made his choice. Each **BEST** that agrees with his will gain five points, each **NEXT BEST** three points. The competitor with the highest number of points will be awarded the grand double prize.

GROUP 1 (Stories)

A Shy Girl in a Sari
B The Wheel-Chair Guide
C The Caravan Campers
D The Telltale Picture

GROUP 2 (Articles)

A Makers of Maps
B Euroflags
C How I Became a Guide
D Anne Frank's House
E "Miss Daisy", Founder of the Girl Scouts
F Guides of a Tropical Island
G Search for the Thames
H Put on Your Own Pantomime
I Out with a Wildlife Photographer

GROUP 3 (Puzzles, Quizzes)

A Morse Code Crossword
B Coin Quiz
C Bird Crossword
D Find the Flowers
E Pathfinder Puzzle
F Flower Quiz

GROUP 4 (8-point Programme)

A Becoming a Homemaker
B Exploring the Arts
C Enjoying the Out-of-Doors

GROUP 5 (How-to-Makes)

A It's a Good Idea
B Sand Castles for the Party
C For Patrol Corner, Home, Camp
D Bead Weaving
E Plaster Flower Pictures
F Novelty Pencil
G Shell Pendants and Necklaces

What I like most about Guiding

THE GIRL GUIDE ANNUAL EXCITING NEW £100 PRIZE COMPETITION

You will enjoy going in for this rewarding competition. Whatever your age, you will have an equal chance of winning the marvellous double prize of a brand-new bicycle and £50 for your Company. If you prefer something else to a bicycle you could have whatever you would like of equal value.

When you have made your choice of titles from the different groups listed on page 47, and marked them on the entry form, think about what you like most about Guiding and write about it in the space provided on page 47. Your write-up shouldn't be more than about fifty words. It will be taken into account if there should be more than one competitor with the same number of winning points, so give it thought and care.

When you have completed both front and back of the entry form, cut it out and post it in an envelope to THE GIRL GUIDE ANNUAL PRIZE COMPETITION, PURNELL BOOKS, BERKSHIRE HOUSE, QUEEN STREET, MAIDENHEAD, BERKSHIRE, SL6 1NF.

Your entry should be sent to arrive not later than March 31st, 1976. The winner will be notified and the prize awarded as soon after this date as possible.

The publishers' decision is final, and no correspondence will be entered into in connection with the competition.

THE GIRL GUIDE ANNUAL £100 COMPETITION ENTRY FORM

Just write down the letter that is set against the title of your choice in the various groups

GROUP 1—(Stories)
BEST . . . . . .
NEXT BEST . . . . . .

GROUP 2—(Articles)
BEST . . . . . .
NEXT BEST . . . . . .

GROUP 3—(Puzzles, Quizzes)
BEST . . . . . .
NEXT BEST . . . . . .

GROUP 4—(8-point Programme)
BEST . . . . . .
NEXT BEST . . . . . .

GROUP 5—(How-to-Makes)
BEST . . . . . .
NEXT BEST . . . . . .

My Name and Address: . . . .
. . . .
My Age: . . . . **My Company:** . . . .
My Guider's Name and Address: . . . .

To Guiders

Contributions of all kinds related to Guiding are welcomed for the *Girl Guide Annual* throughout the year.

Colour slides or prints and black-and-white photographs are also required. These should be briefly and factually described and bear the name and address of the sender.

Please send all contributions with stamped and fully addressed envelope to THE EDITOR, GUIDING ANNUALS, PURNELL BOOKS, BERKSHIRE HOUSE, QUEEN STREET, MAIDENHEAD, BERKSHIRE, SL6 1NF.

Payment for contributions and photographs is made soon after acceptance.

Becoming a Homemaker

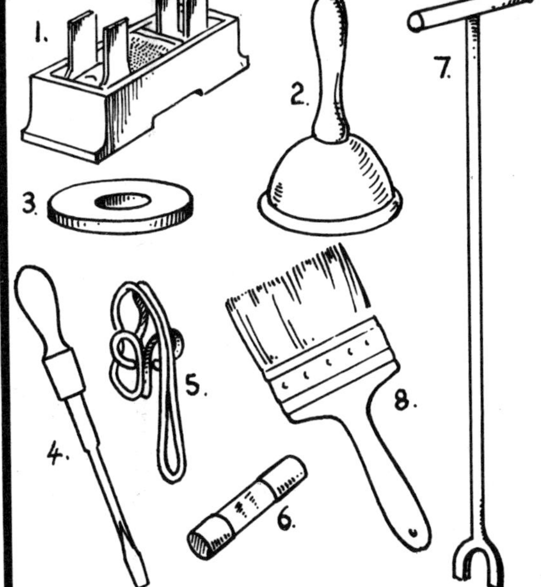

WHAT ARE THESE THINGS? WHAT WOULD YOU DO WITH THEM?

HOW MANY JOBS CAN YOU SEE NEEDING DOING? COULD YOU DO THEM?

AS A GOOD HOSTESS? WHAT WOULD YOU DO WITH THESE TO MAKE YOUR GUEST FEEL WELCOME?

COOKING THESE FOODS, WHICH CONTAINER WOULD YOU USE FOR EACH?

ROSALIE M BROWN

PATHFINDER PUZZLE

By J. M. Sylvester

Answer the clues below with one word and you will find that the first letter of each spells out a longer word.

CLUES

1. Guides and Scouts are always this
2. A beast of burden
3. You could follow this through the woods
4. Aeroplanes are kept in these
5. The Union Jack is one
6. Natives of North America
7. You would not be able to smell without it
8. You sometimes do this when you are asleep
9. The capital city of Scotland
10. It is used to steer a boat

S.O.S.

by Jean Howard

Mandy went canoeing,
Saw an island close at hand,
Decided she would rest there
For a while, then back to land.

Mandy started dozing,
Woke to find her boat had gone
And the sea had only left a patch
Of sand to stand upon!

Mandy used her paddles,
Sent a signal to the shore;
If you want to know the message
You must learn your semaphore.

A kindly coastguard saw her,
Read the message, rang a bell,
Sent the lifeboat out to fetch her,
And the ending? All was well!

ALL ABOUT ANNE

by A. L. Blowers

The missing word in each sentence contains the word ANNE.

1. Anne says that smoking is . . . . . . in her home.
2. Anne says that . . . . . . food is not as good as fresh.
3. Anne and her Patrol . . . . an exciting expedition.
4. Anne helped to carry the . . . . . . in a procession.
5. Anne had to sleep in the . . . . . . as the hotel was full.
6. Anne . . . . . . the embers into a blazing camp-fire.
7. Anne found that the boat was . . . . . . by a good crew.
8. Anne returned from camp . . . . . . by the sun.
9. Anne's family are spending a holiday in the south of France at . . . . . .
10. Anne's grandfather . . . . . . for gold in Australia.

Exploring the Arts

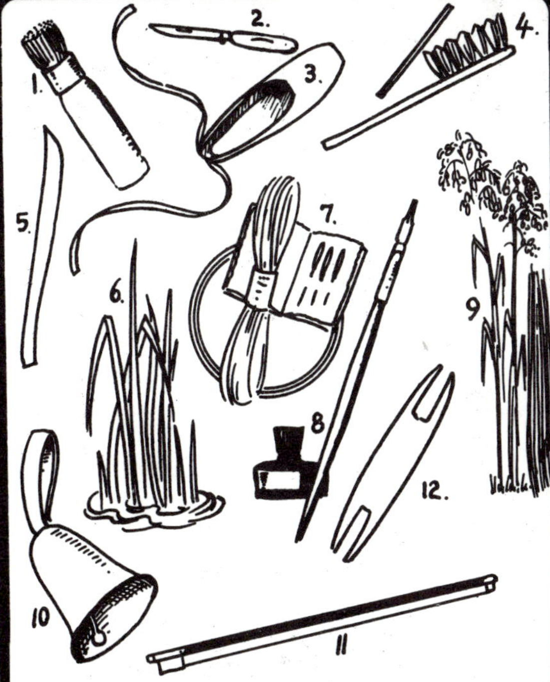

SOME OBJECTS USED IN EXPLORING THE ARTS. WHAT ARE THEY USED FOR?

CAN YOU SAY WHERE IN THE WORLD YOU WOULD FIND THESE ARTS?

1. THE SECRET CLOCK
2. WUTHERING WILLOWS
3. THE PREJUDICE MILL
4. CHILD'S GARDEN OF STORIES
5. UNCLE TOM'S GARDEN
6. DAVID ON THE FLOSS
7. THE WIND IN THE CABIN
8. THE LADY OF THE VERSES
9. THE CUCKOO LOOKING-GLASS
10. JUST SO COPPERFIELD
11. ALICE THROUGH THE LAKE
12. PRIDE AND HEIGHTS

CAN YOU SORT OUT THESE MIXED-UP BOOK TITLES? NAME THE AUTHORS.

WEARING THESE HEAD-DRESSES WHEN ACTING, WHICH COUNTRIES WOULD YOU REPRESENT?

Enjoying the Out-of-Doors

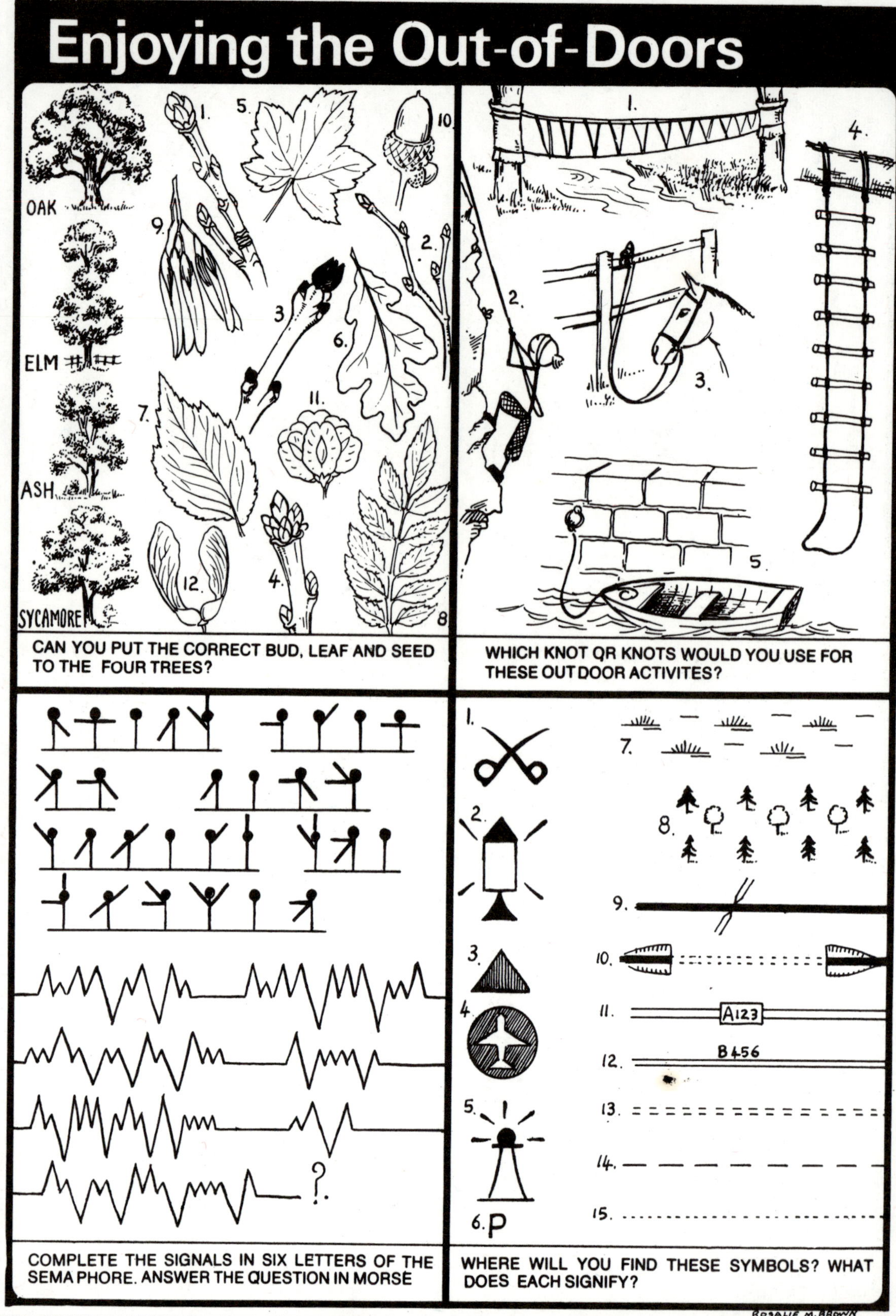

The CARAVAN CAMPERS

by Winifred M. Peppin

The 2nd Sutton Company were very fortunate. Their Guider had recently bought a trailer caravan, which slept five. As the Assistant Guider possessed an old Dormobile, they had a really splendid set-up.

The caravan was parked in a corner of a field on a farm a few miles out of town. In the summer the Company were going, Patrol by Patrol, to spend a week in it, with one of the Guiders residing nearby in the Dormobile.

Their Guider told them, "It's not to be just a holiday—I'll expect you to work for your badges."

They did too—Naturalist, Bird-Watcher, Agility, Athlete, Map Reader, and Rambler—and it was all great fun. Even the unfortunate Guides who struck bad weather were able to practise for Homemaker, although in rather cramped conditions.

It was the turn of the Wren Patrol, and an excited group of girls surged out of the laden Dormobile as they reached their destination.

Miss Harris, the Assistant Guider, unlocked the caravan door. Soon there was a babble of voices.

"Two beds in this little room."

"And two bunks in this tiny one."

"Bags I the top bunk!"

"But there are only four beds!"

"Now, wait a minute," said Miss Harris. "Here's the fifth one, right here in the living-room." She flipped the narrow settee, and there was the fifth bed! "For the first night, you had better draw lots for the beds," she went on. "After that, those who want to swop can arrange it between themselves. Lorna, will you see to it?"

Lorna tore a page of her notebook into five equal pieces, folded them, put them into her cap, and shook it. "Now each take one," she said.

"Oh, good!" said Beth. "Joan and I have the bunks—and I'm in the top one!"

"I'm glad I'm not up there," said Joan, who was the youngest Guide. "I'd be afraid of falling out in the night."

"I've got the best of all," said Peggy, "the living-room, all to myself!"

"That's a good thing!" said Alice.

"Why?" Peggy looked at the Second rather suspiciously.

"Because you're so untidy and careless. Now you'll *have* to put your things away; we don't want this room in a mess. It will be good training for you."

"Oh!" said Peggy thoughtfully. Then she said, "Lorna, as P.L., shouldn't you have this lovely room to yourself?"

"I wouldn't think of depriving you of it," said Lorna, laughing. "Cheer up, Peggy! There's a cupboard here where you can put your things."

"And the bedding goes in this locker under the seat," added Miss Harris.

"I've only got a sleeping-bag—that won't be much trouble," said Peggy cheerfully.

They all set to and unpacked the Dormobile. Then Peggy and Joan went over to the farm for milk and eggs. A girl of about Joan's age came to the door.

"Another bunch of bluebirds!"

A girl of about Joan's age came to the door.

she said, rather unpleasantly.

"Now, that will do, Tammy!" Her mother, a comfortable-looking woman, came to the door. "You're from the caravan, aren't you? I've got your milk and eggs here ready. If you run out of anything else, just come up and I'll see what I can do for you. We've got some nice fresh lettuces in the garden—radishes, too."

"Thank you, Mrs Martin," said Peggy. "I think we should have some of each. We all like salads.'

While Tammy was getting the lettuce and radishes, Joan made friends with a beautiful Persian cat.

"That's my cat," said Tammy on her return. She pushed the salad stuff at Peggy, then snatched the cat away and went into the house.

Joan looked very hurt.

"Nasty little beast!" said Peggy. "Never mind her."

That evening round the campfire they discussed what they were going to work at. Lorna and Beth were keen on gaining the Bird-Watcher badge.

"Would you like to join them Joan?" asked Miss Harris.

"I'd rather look for wild-flowers for my collection," said Joan, rather shyly.

"Yes, that is about all you need now before taking your Naturalist test, isn't it? What are you two going to do?"

"Rope bridges and handstands for me!" said Peggy.

"Oh, the Agility badge! Yes, that should work off some of your surplus energy," said Miss Harris, smiling. "And you, Alice?"

"The same as Peggy. I've got to practise throwing a lifeline, too."

"I'll show you." Peggy was the champion lifeline thrower.

So they divided into groups for part of the time each day. Lorna had brought her little portable tape-recorder with her, and she and Beth, and often Miss Harris, too, would record the bird-songs from wood or field.

Peggy and Alice got on extremely well. Alice was determined to do the things which came so easily to Peggy, and Peggy, who was very good-natured, never tired of showing Alice the best way to do them. Alice didn't manage to throw the lifeline as well as Peggy did. She helped Peggy in many ways, though, and the Patrol noticed that Peggy was not so untidy or careless as she used to be.

Round the campfire they discussed what they were going to work at.

"What do you want those things for?"

Joan, who was rather a solitary girl, wandered happily about by herself, gathering specimens not only of flowers but of leaves and the bark of trees. She pressed the flowers between sheets of blotting-paper inside an old telephone-directory she had brought with her for that purpose, and weighted it down with big flat stones from a nearby stream. The leaves went under the living-room carpet, and she told everyone to walk as much as possible over them. It was just the kind of life she loved, and it would have been perfect if it were not for Tammy.

Tammy had guessed that Joan was sensitive and rather timid, and not being either of these herself she tried to make Joan feel uncomfortable whenever they met. Joan began to think that Tammy often went out of her way to make sure that they *did* meet. Joan had found a field so high up the hill that all kinds of little mountain-flowers grew there. She loved these tiny flowers best of all. There were milkwort and thyme, eyebright, and a tiny scabious which she had never seen before and would have to look up.

She was sitting on the short, fine grass, arranging the flowers in her specimen box, when a voice said, "What do you want those things for?"

"I'm making a collection," replied Joan, too happy to remember how unpleasant Tammy could be. "I press them when I get back to the caravan, and when we go home I shall mount them in my album."

"Huh!" said Tammy. "I've got better things to do than pick somebody else's wildflowers. My dad doesn't like you traipsing all over our land."

Joan remembered that Mr Martin had said that they could go anywhere except on the growing crops. "I know by this time that Guides always close gates after them," he had said.

Tammy was watching her. When she saw that Joan was smiling again, she said, "Don't see why that field you've got the caravan in should be wasted. I'm going to turn the bull into it one of these days."

Peggy would have said, "I'd like to see *you* lead that bull to our field!" But Peggy wasn't there, and Joan was terrified of cows, let alone bulls. She picked up the specimen-box and walked away.

Tammy shouted after her, "You'd better look round before you go out of the caravan or you might get a surprise some day!"

Joan was so quiet that evening that the others teased her until they saw that she was really upset; then they coaxed her until she told them what was worrying her.

"That Tammy!" Peggy jumped to her feet. "I'll fix her!"

"She won't do it, of course," said Lorna to Joan.

"I know that, but all the same I keep looking to see if the bull is there," said Joan miserably.

"I think we should tell Mr Martin how she is behaving," said Alice.

"You know," said Beth, thoughtfully, "I think she is really jealous of the good time we have, and would like to join in, but because she started all wrong she won't give in and make friends."

"Is that it?" Joan brightened up. "Then I won't let her worry me any more. Don't tell Miss Harris or Mr Martin. Why, I feel *sorry* for her now."

"We won't say anything if you will be sure to tell us if she's beastly again," Lorna promised.

But it was Tammy who was frightened the next day. Joan was working her way through a meadow, gathering as many different kinds of buttercup as she could find, when she heard the bull bellowing in the next field.

Peggy explained how Tammy was to slide her feet along the lower rope while she held on to the top one.

She was not very worried, for there was a strong fence between the fields; but then she heard a scream and, looking up, saw Tammy running as fast as she could towards the dividing fence. The bull, snorting and with his head down, was galloping after her.

"She'll never make it,' thought Joan.

Not knowing what to do, she picked up a large branch and ran to the fence, but before she reached it Tammy streaked like a frightened cat up a nearby tree. The bull pawed the ground underneath it, and made angry rumbling noises.

"Are you all right?" called Joan.

"Yes, but he'll never let me get down."

"I'll run up to the farm and get your father."

"That'd be no use. It's market-day and they've all gone to town. They left me to look after the baby chicks."

"Then what were you doing down here?"

"I wanted to see what you were doing. I didn't know the bull was here—he must have broken the fence of the bull-yard. What *were* you doing? You were zigzagging all over the field!"

"I was seeing how many kinds of buttercup I could find."

"There's only one kind, isn't there?"

Joan laughed. "No, there are lots. I'll show you if you like, but we've got to get you down

from that tree first. Hold on and I'll run and get Peggy and Alice. They were in the caravan field when I left."

She ran back to the field. Sure enough, Peggy was still showing Alice how to throw a lifeline.

"Bring your line, too, Alice," said Peggy, hastily coiling up her own.

The three girls ran up to the meadow. The bull muttered angrily at them, but stayed beneath the tree. Tammy looked down at them anxiously.

"I've got to get down. The baby chicks will need feeding," she said.

"Pity you ever left them," said Peggy, unfeelingly.

Alice said to Peggy, "This tree on our side—would a lifeline reach from it to Tammy's tree?"

"We'll soon find out. Get ready to catch the rope, Tammy."

Peggy made a perfect throw. Tammy lunged at it and nearly fell out of the tree, but managed to save herself and grasp the end of the rope.

"Tie it up to a branch with a bowline knot," ordered Peggy. "Oh, you don't know what a bowline is." She stood on the fence and explained how a bowline should be tied.

Alice was in the tree on the other side of the fence, tying her end level with Tammy's.

"I'm not walking over that!" declared Tammy.

"There's another one coming—catch!" Peggy threw the other rope. "Now tie it to that branch exactly above the first one. Can you get up there?"

The second line was fixed, and Peggy explained how Tammy was to slide her feet along the lower rope while she held on to the top one. But Tammy refused to try.

"Suppose the ropes break?" she wailed.

"I'll come over and show you.' Peggy went up the first tree, and was soon crossing on the rope. The bull roared up at her.

"I daren't go while the bull is there," cried Tammy.

"The idea is," said Peggy, "that you go precisely because the bull *is* there. There would be no point in all this if he was in the barn."

Down below, Joan saw that Tammy was too terrified to try to cross. "Wait!" she called. Then she picked up the long branch she had found earlier and, leaning over the fence, poked at the bull with it.

They all gasped at the sight of the timid Joan teasing a bull. He turned to her with a roar, and Joan ran along the side of the fence away from the tree. While the bull chased along on his side, Peggy persuaded Tammy to inch along the rope until Alice could reach out and grab her. Then, when Joan had lured the bull to the corner of the field, Peggy untied the ropes, dropped to the ground, and ran for the fence.

The bull came back, but he was much too late.

"We'd better help you with those chickens," said Alice to Tammy.

Tammy was gazing open-mouthed at Peggy. "You climbed down that tree and ran across! Gosh, you are brave!"

"Brave nothing!" snorted Peggy. "That bull was far enough off—thanks to Joan. *She* was the brave one!"

Tammy thought a bit. Then she said, "Yes, she was the bravest of all—and she's scared of bulls, too, isn't she? I'm sorry I was so horrid to you, Joan. Do you think I could join the Guides—and be in your Patrol?"

Bead Weaving

by Walter J. Smith

Have you ever admired the beautiful glass beadwork that comes from the Far East? You can make belts and necklaces of beads on a simple, age-old type of loom.

It costs very little. All you need is a stout cardboard box, two combs, and a reel of stout thread.

Look at Illustration No. 1. This shows a fairly long box cut well down on each side, but not enough to weaken it. There is a comb, mounted teeth up, at each end and held in place with sticky tape.

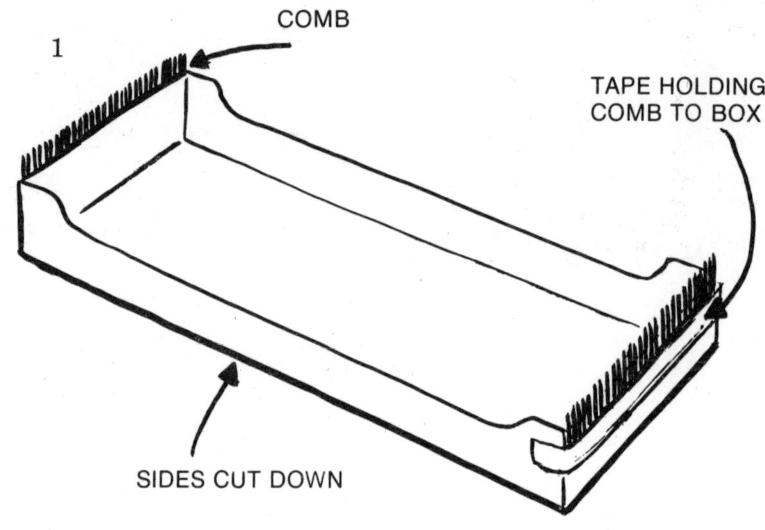

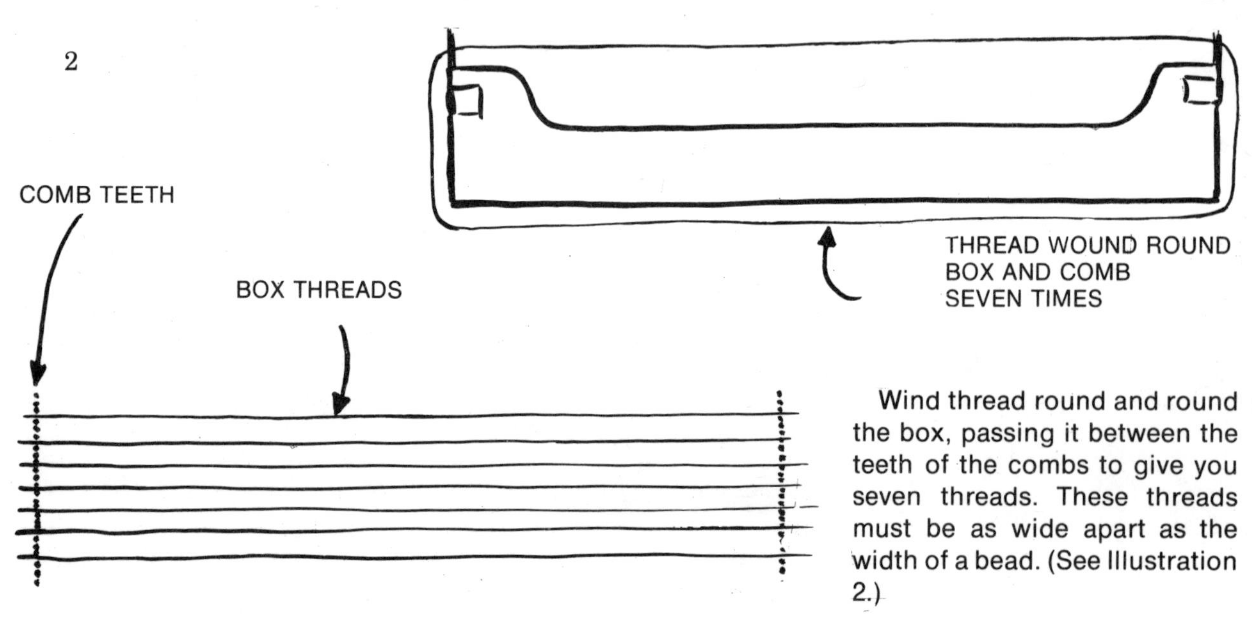

Wind thread round and round the box, passing it between the teeth of the combs to give you seven threads. These threads must be as wide apart as the width of a bead. (See Illustration 2.)

Now thread a needle fine enough to go through your beads and fasten one end to the box near a comb. Then run six beads onto your needle and push them down onto the thread. Take your needle and push it *under* the threads on the box, and holding the cotton either side pull the beads upwards so that there is a box thread on either side of each bead. (See Illustration 3.)

BEADS LIFTED INTO POSITION

3

THREAD RUNS UNDER BOX THREADS

Now bring your needle *above* the threads on the box and run it through the beads, again making sure the thread passes *over* the threads on the box. This of course means there is a length of thread going both sides of the threads on the box and so locking the beads into position. (See Illustration 4.)

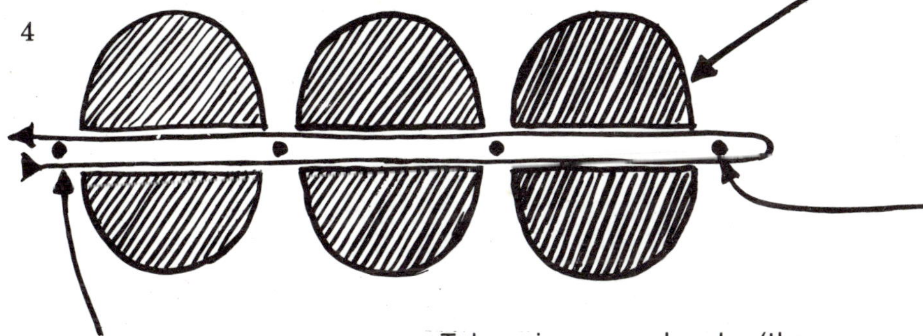

BEADS DRAWN TO SHOW HOLES

END VIEW OF A BOX THREAD

NEEDLE THREAD SHOWN GOING THROUGH BEADS FIRST UNDER, THEN OVER BOX THREADS

Take six more beads (the same or different colours, according to what pattern you want) and do the same thing all over again. This gives you two rows of beads next to each other. Carry on and you will find the length grows very quickly. The lines of beads must be pushed well up to one another.

When you have finished, turn your loom over and snip the threads through in the middle. Gather them up each end, as near to the beads as possible, and tie round at that point with a piece of thread. It helps to put a spot of gum on the knot. You can plait the rest of the loose ends together, if you like. You can then use these to tie the ornament in position.

All sorts of beads can be used—glass, wood, plastic, even your own rolled-paper ones. But the glass type always look particularly effective.

How I Became a Guide

by Pamela Phillips

At the first meeting there was a barbecue

My lifelong ambition was to become a Girl Guide. I went to boarding-school when I was nine years old and thought that I would become a Guide immediately. But I had to be a Brownie for two years. My eleventh birthday was on a Tuesday, and I went to my first Guide meeting the following evening. Looking back, I think it was the prospect of staying up until half-past seven instead of being pushed upstairs at five o'clock, that must have been the main attraction, together with the simple supper we were allowed after the meeting.

We were quite an ordinary Company except that we were spastics. At that first meeting there was a barbecue in the grounds of our school, and despite the rain which had been falling all day it was very successful. When the wood had been collected for the fire I was given the job of breaking it up. As it was damp and I was lying on the wet ground to do it, I must have looked a spectacle. The housemother reprimanded me for getting the clean dress I had put on especially for the meeting so dirty. For the barbecue we had sausages, which were burnt to a cinder, potatoes which were half boiled, and bread and butter which someone had conveniently left in a pool of water. Needless to say, we all enjoyed ourselves!

I was determined that my Guide career would be triumphant because as a Brownie I had been a dismal failure—at least, I thought so. Luckily, I am blessed with a good memory and was able to repeat my Promise and Law parrot-fashion to my Captain within a few weeks. Doing knots was my stumbling-block, partly because my hands did not function properly and partly because I am not practical-minded. The learning and passing of my knots test was finally accomplished with the encouragement and bullying of my Patrol Leader. I was enrolled by the District Commissioner, which was considered a great honour.

Another important event during my early Guiding days was the winning of the Badge of Fortitude by one of our senior Guides. Although she could not walk, talk or use her hands, she not only gained her Second and First Class badges, she was the only spastic Guide to achieve her All Round Cords, which was the last test before the Queen's Guide badge. This is the pinnacle for the Extension Guide.

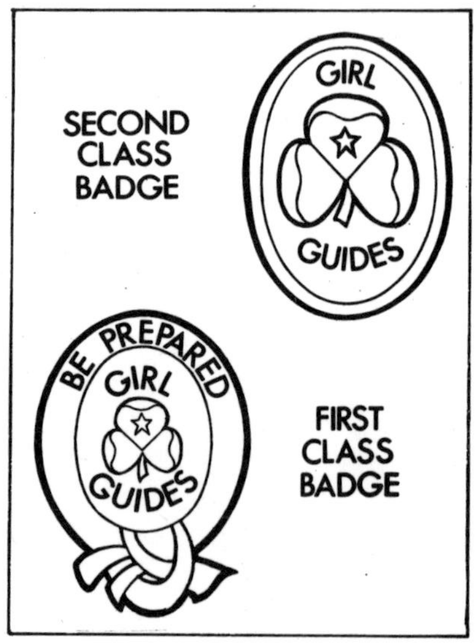

Obtaining Second Class and First Class badges was a long process for the disabled Guide. Bedmaking was for me the most arduous task. For one week I had to strip and make my own bed under the eagle eye of a friend who was expert at making beds. The stripping was accomplished quite easily; I could even lay the blanket back on the bed, but when it came to tucking in the sheet I was hopeless; the envelope corners were my bugbear; although I did them as I was instructed, they would simply fall open when I tried to tuck them in. I was glad when that week was over.

A nursing career was unattainable for me, so I decided to do the next best alternative and achieve the three Guide proficiency badges for Child Nurse, Sick Nurse and First Aid. Child Nurse was the first I tackled. I mastered the theory, but when it came to the practical I met my Waterloo. Always finding little boys more amenable than girls, I asked if I could look after one of the male infants of our school under the supervision of my housemother. He turned out to be a little demon. When I had displayed a wide selection of toys, games and books in one of the classrooms I invited him in. Surely, one game or toy in my collection would interest him, I thought. Taking him by the hand, which was rather like taking an unruly dog on a lead, I proceeded to entertain him. Toy engines had no appeal for him, nor had the big red motor-car. I tried a game of hide-and-seek to no avail. His main objective was running to the door and trying to squeeze through it before I could reach him. Our afternoon's entertainment became a nightmare in which I endeavoured to reach the door before he did. As he could run faster than me, I was worn out by teatime. I think I passed my Child Nurse badge for my endurance rather than for my Child Nurse qualities!

After about two years in my first Company I changed schools and consequently Companies. This Company was newly formed. To my astonishment, I became a Patrol Leader almost immediately. Our Company was assisted by the local Rangers. We were so grateful for their help that when they went to Switzerland we held a handcraft sale on our school open day and raised twenty-five pounds towards their holiday, which they really appreciated.

My crowning achievement in my second Guide Company was attaining my First Class badge, which was presented to me by England's Extension Adviser

His main objective was running to the door before I could reach him

Make Plaster Flower Pictures

Andrew Liston Shows You How

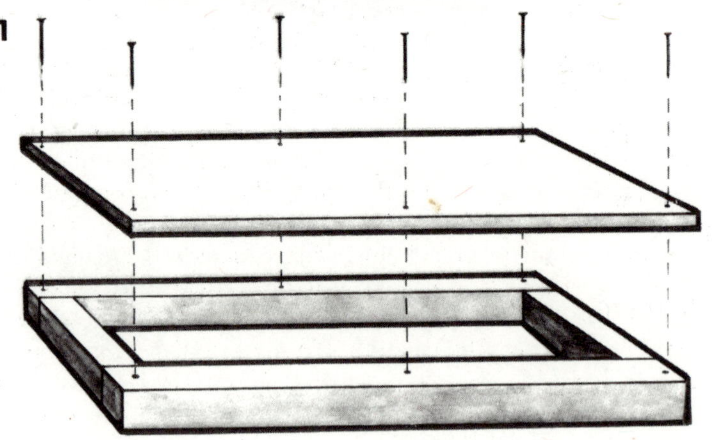

Flower studies in plaster make charming and unusual wall-decorations and are easy to make. The raised plaster flowers and leaves stand out realistically from their background, and the jewel-like colours glow against the dark ground colour.

Fig. 1. All that you need to make one of these panels is a piece of hardboard about four times as long as it is wide—61cm (24″) × 15·2cm (6″), for example—and enough woodstrip to go round the edge of the hardboard. The thickness of the woodstrip does not matter greatly; it should be 2cm (¾″) thick or more, for its main purpose is to stop the hardboard from warping.

Glue a strip down the back of the hardboard, flush with its edges, then nail the strips down with 2cm-long panel-pins hammered in about 2·5cm (1″) apart.

Next, glue in a top and bottom strip to fill the spaces between the side strips, then use panel-pins to secure these in place.

Fig. 2. Cover the front and sides of the panel with oil paint into which a little dry sand has been stirred to make it rough. The colour does not matter. Put the paint on thickly, dabbing it rather than stroking it on. If necessary, apply a second coat so that the surface of the panel is rough enough to give the plaster a good grip.

Fig. 3. Choose a plant as a model. Pictures in plant and flower catalogues, and those in reference books of flowers, can be used for this. Include a leaf as well as at least one flower. Draw them on the panel, making them as large as possible without touching the edges.

Fig. 4. Mix some plaster-filler with just enough water to make a stiff paste, and spread it with a knife over the shapes you have drawn on the panel. The plaster should be at least ·3cm

(⅛″) thick. Plaster-of-paris will give a whiter finish than plaster-filler, and the finished flowers will be slightly more brilliant, but it sets very quickly. If you are going to use plaster-of-paris, mix only enough for one flower or leaf at a time. Leave the surface of the flowers quite rough. Use the knife-blade to mark the veins of the leaves and the folds of the petals.

Fig. 5. To make the stems, trail a stick dipped in plaster along the pencilled guide-line. This may have to be done several times, until the stem projects enough.

Fig. 6. When the plaster is dry, colour in the flowers and leaves. A brilliant finish can be obtained by using waterproof drawing-inks, but water-colour paints or poster-colours can also be used. One point to watch is that in order to cover the leaf completely, especially in its indentations, the colour will mark the background; this does not matter. Make sure that all the plaster shapes are covered by looking at them from different angles, then leave the panel to dry.

Fig. 7. Use a small water-colour brush to paint the background in a dark colour. Oil paint, emulsion paint or indian ink can be used for this. Paint the sides as well as the face. Make sure that the paint is applied very carefully round the plant, especially at the stems. When it has dried, your panel is ready to hang.

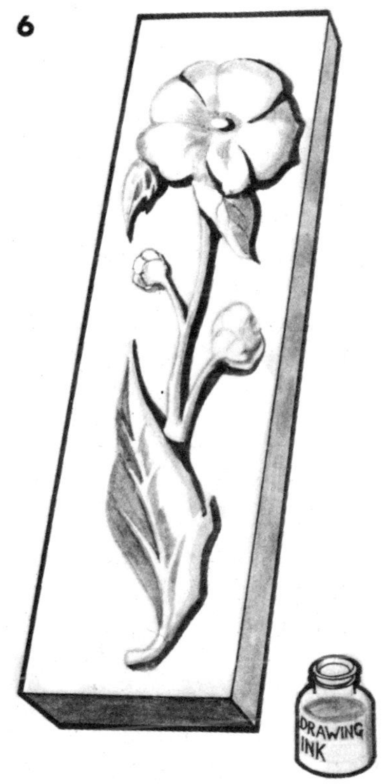

8.

6. In Devon they call it a "butter rose", but its usual name comes from the Latin word for first. Where would you look for this spring flower?
7. Which spring flower found in damp places was dedicated to the Virgin Mary and known as "Mary's Gold"?
8. Why do we associate a particular flower with March 1st?

flower quiz

Set and photographed by Doris Nicholson

1. What wild flower do you associate with November 11th? Do you know why it was chosen to represent this day?
2. There is an old saying that "Kissing's not in season when . . . . . is not in bloom". Can you fill in the missing flower?
3. According to Greek mythology the god of the west wind caused the death of a young man who was a favourite of the sun god, Apollo. Apollo caused his friend to live again in the form of a spring flower. What was the young man's name, and what do we usually call the flower? (Be careful not to confuse it with its Scottish namesake.)
4. This cruciform flower is grown commercially to produce pods to make a condiment for the table.
5. It is said that spring has not arrived until you can put your foot on twelve of these flowers at once. What are they?

6.

4
1
3
GGA-E

LEARNING and HELPING

Photo: **Miss Stella Ball**

Wycombe Guides help old people shop in a local department store at Christmas by pushing them round in wheel-chairs

Learnings about cars
Photo: ***L. D. Curtis***

Make a Novelty Pencil

Daphne M. Pilcher Shows You How to Make a Guide Badge Decoration for a Pencil

All you need is a little yellow felt and some black cotton. Felt is the best material for this activity because it does not fray.

1. Using the outline below, cut out the outline of two yellow badges.
2. With sharp scissors cut out pieces marked A and B.
3. Mark the Gs on the felt lightly with pencil, then fill them in on both badges with chain-stitch in black cotton.
4. Lightly marking in the part shown by the broken line, sew both badges together with back-stitch. Before completing, check that your size of pencil 'will fit into it. Don't forget the part marked C must be left open for inserting the pencil.
5. Finish off by blanket-stitching the outside of the two badges together.

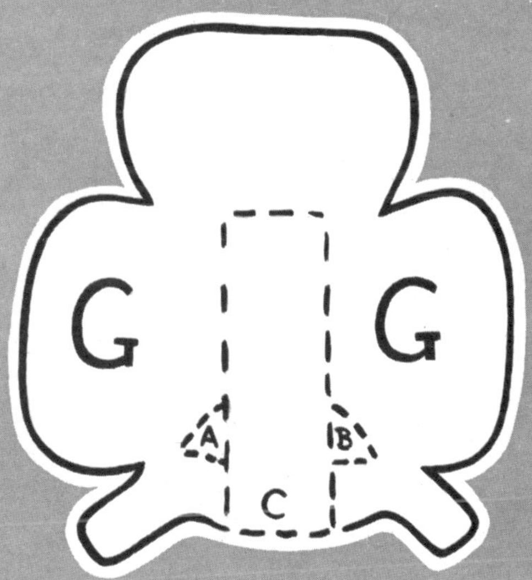

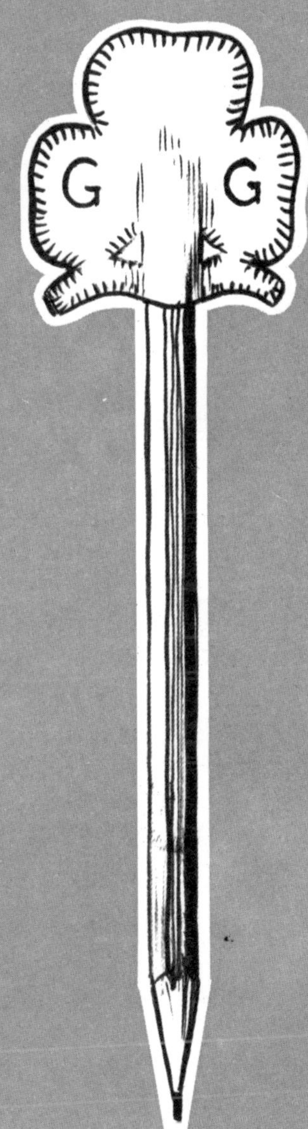

The finished article

Camp tuckshop of the 2nd Maidenhead (St. Luke's) Guides

Colour slide by **Miss Marian Hutchin**

Random snapshots of the 1st Bishopston Company, Swansea, in camp near Builth Wells

Candid Camera

Water suppliers

One-girl stores transport

Packed up and ready to go home

olour slides by **Mrs M. Booth**

ANNE FRANK'S HOUSE

Not far from the centre of Amsterdam, alongside a canal, stands a row of tall houses. I stood and looked at them with Guides of the 10th Chiswick (St. Nicholas') Company. The ground floors are used as shops, small workshops or store-rooms. These houses have been like this for many years, but during the last war one of them sheltered a small group of Jews, among them Anne Frank, a girl of sixteen, and her mother and family.

When the Germans occupied Amsterdam they began to harass the Jews in the same way as in their own country. Many Jews were sent to concentration camps and the gas chambers. But the man who owned one of the row of tall houses and ran a small printing workshop on the lower floors was a friend of many Jews. He decided to help some of them if he could, although he knew that the penalty, if he was caught, was death.

Anne and her family moved in after dark. They were taken through a secret door concealed behind a bookcase in an office on the second floor and led to an apartment of four rooms on the top floor of an annexe, or "backhouse", which they later shared with four other people.

Anne Frank's house from the outside

by V. Hinton

During the day they had to keep very quiet. They could not cook a meal, as there was only a small coal-stove, and if smoke rose from the chimney someone might see it and become suspicious. If they moved around, someone in the workshop might hear them.

The windows were covered by thick net curtains so that anyone looking out of the windows of houses backing on to the one Anne was living in could not see the people secreted there. Even at night Anne and her family had to be careful. No light must show, and they still could not make a noise. Food was brought to them by the owner of the house.

Many months passed, and Anne passed her time by keeping a diary. In it she wrote down all her thoughts, her hopes that the war would end soon, and her thoughts on the sort of world she hoped it would be in the future. But always there was the fear that she and her family would be betrayed. Sometimes she almost wished that this would happen so that the awful confinement in these upper rooms would end.

Eventually a workman in the printing works became suspicious. He heard a noise upstairs when he came back to the works one night. He told the Gestapo.

The soldiers came and took Anne and her family to a concentration camp, where Anne died just before the end of the war.

Her father survived and found her diary. It was published in book form in many languages, and a film was made of Anne's secret life in the top rooms of the tall house.

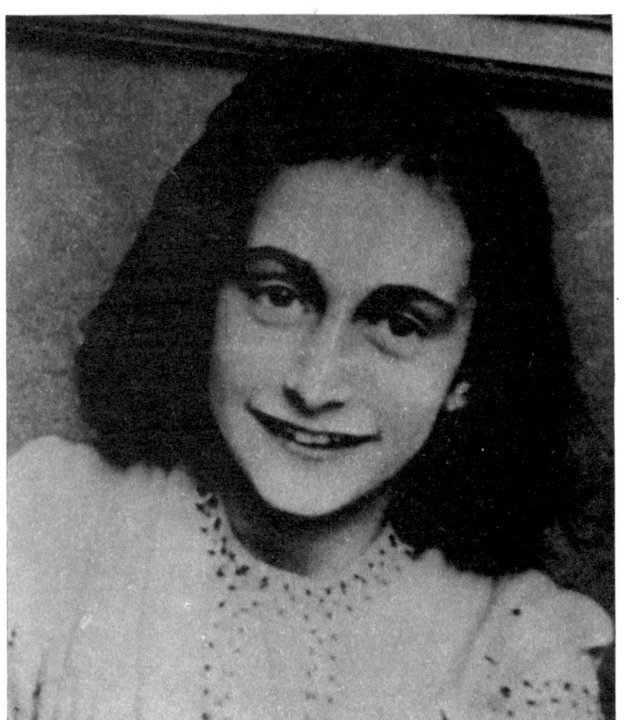

Anne Frank

The room in Anne Frank's house with the bookcase hiding the entrance to the "backhouse" or annexe in which the Frank family lived in secret

The secret entrance behind the bookcase, which was hooked to the wall and could only be moved if unfastened from inside

Today these rooms are preserved just as they were then. The printing shop is still in active existence. People come from all over the world to see Anne Frank's house. The profits from the sale of the book go to promote international friendship.

Guides

Guides of the 5th Sunbury Company find themselves sharing breakfast with an unexpected guest

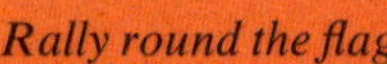

Rally round the flag

Guides of the 2nd Shepperton Company make a sedan-chair as a camp challenge – and use it!

Colour slides by Miss A. M. Stevens

The uninvited camper

at Camp

Makers of Maps

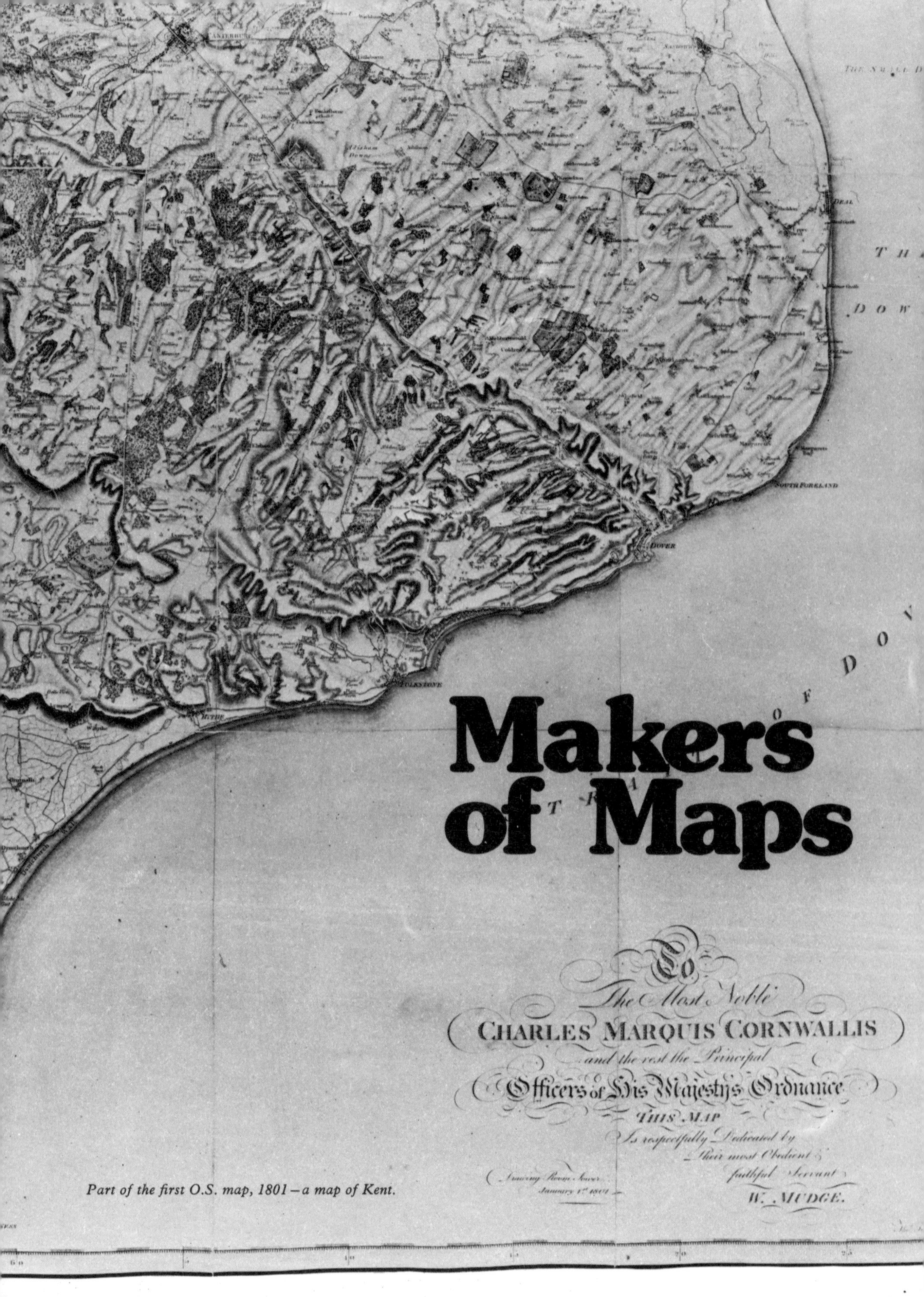

Part of the first O.S. map, 1801 – a map of Kent.

The first Ordnance Survey map appeared in January, 1801; it covered the County of Kent at a scale of one inch to the mile, and was printed in black-and-white by a process known as copper engraving. It is not surprising that the thoughts of the map-makers turned at that time to the coastal country facing France. In 1799, after many years of war, Napoleon had made himself supreme ruler of France; nobody in England imagined that the French wars were over and there was always a possibility that Napoleon would succeed in crossing the Channel and invade England. The map of Kent and those which immediately followed it were therefore intended for the defence of the country. The drawing of the map was done in the Tower of London, where the offices of the Ordnance Survey were situated.

The next stage was the copper engraving. First the line work of the drawing was transferred by hand to a sheet of copper; then the engraver cut into the copper, following the transferred lines. He also had to engrave all the names, writing each name backwards in mirror image. Prints were made by rubbing greasy ink into the engraved lines and pressing the sheets of paper very firmly against the copper plate by means of a press so that the ink was transferred to the paper.

The Ordnance Survey had been officially formed ten years earlier, in 1791, as a small department under the Board of Ordnance, hence the name by which it has since been known. In those days the Honourable Board of Ordnance was a large and important department responsible for fortifications and armaments and everything connected with them. In the middle of the nineteenth century the Board of Ordnance was abolished and the control of the Ordnance Survey passed to the War Office. After many similar changes, it is today the responsibility of the Department of the Environment. The Ordnance Survey remained in the Tower for fifty years until, in October, 1841, a disastrous fire occurred which resulted in much damage to its offices and to its equipment. A new home had to be found, and at that time there happened to be some empty buildings in Southampton which had originally been used as a cavalry barracks. Into these buildings the Ordnance Survey was moved and it remained there until 1968, when its new headquarters, also in Southampton, was finished.

When the Napoleonic wars were over, the need for military maps became less important. However, the value of maps for civil purposes was realised by many people, and one of the results of this growing interest was a demand for much more detail to be shown. This made it necessary to survey the country at a larger scale. First the six-inch-to-the-mile scale was adopted, printed in black-and-white, like the map of Kent, from copper plates, but in 1855 it was decided to produce an even larger scale of map—twenty-five inches to the mile—which showed buildings and fences in great detail and much other information besides. By the end of the century the whole country (except for areas of mountain and moorland) was covered by these very large-scale maps, and Great Britain became the best mapped country in the world. The main use of the large-scale maps in the nineteenth century was for buying and selling land and for the management of land; there were many other uses, which have perhaps become more important in recent times, such as for planning and

The fire at the Tower of London, in which were the offices of the Ordnance Survey until 1841

by W. A. Seymour—Ordnance Survey

for engineering. The twenty-five-inch maps were not engraved on copper but were printed by lithography. In this process a flat stone or a slightly roughened sheet of zinc is used as the printing surface. Greasy ink lines are drawn on the stone or zinc and the rest of the surface is kept wet. Consequently when an inky roller is passed over the stone or metal sheet the greasy lines are freshly charged with ink but the wet areas remain clean. Prints are made by pressing sheets of paper against the stone or metal.

In the nineteenth century the surveyors, who at that time were mostly soldiers, had no motor transport and no aeroplanes or helicopters. They had to rely on horses, mules, and very largely on their own feet. There is one account of a party of surveyors in Scotland who walked nearly six hundred miles in twenty-two days,

A surveyor using a theodolite to measure angles from an O.S. triangulation pillar

A surveyor at work with a Tellurometer, which operates by the use of a radio wave

A rotary machine on which maps are printed at speed

A stereo plotting machine, on which a floating mark is coupled to a pen that automatically draws the true position of a feature on a map

mostly from hilltop to hilltop. The nights were often spent under canvas, especially when working in the more remote parts of the country. The instruments they used were large and heavy and had either to be hauled in carts or carried to the tops of the hills. Nevertheless, all the twenty-five-inch-to-the-mile maps were completed in about forty years—a very remarkable achievement.

The job of making a map is always divided into two parts; these resemble the stages in the construction of some large buildings. First of all, a framework has to be made, comparable with the steel-girder framework of the building, and then all the map detail has to be fitted within this framework in the same manner as the walls, floors, plumbing and electrical cables are added to the building. In both map and building the framework holds everything in place. The framework of a map is usually made by triangulation – that is, by the measurement of a network of triangles covering the whole of the area to be mapped. The network is made up of large triangles which are subdivided successively into smaller and smaller triangles. The lengths of a few of the shorter sides are measured, as are all of the angles in all of the triangles. It is possible from this information to calculate the lengths of all the sides of the triangles. In the nineteenth century, except in the more remote areas, the smallest set of triangles had sides between one and two miles long.

The second stage was carried out by surveyors equipped with chains. Each chain was twenty-two yards long and was divided into a hundred links. The surveyors began by chaining the sides of each of the triangles – the measurements had to agree with the calculated lengths just mentioned – they then added other chain lines across the triangles, continuing in the same way until each triangle was divided by a large number of chain lines. The features of the map – the buildings, fences, roads, etc. – were fixed by "offsets" from the chain lines – that is, by measured distances at right-angles to the chain lines at particular recorded points on them. Finally, the triangles and chain lines were drawn to scale and the features of the map were plotted from the offsets. Compared with the methods used today, the chain survey was slow and laborious, making the accomplishment of the nineteenth-century surveyors even more striking.

All went well until the First World War (1914-1918), when most of the surveyors and draughtsmen were sent to France. After the war there was an economic depression, and the size of the Ordnance Survey was severely reduced. As a result, the maps became more and more out of date until in many places they were of little use. Just before the outbreak of the Second World War, a start was made on the large task of bringing the maps up to date and making new maps where necessary. This job of restoration is still going on and will not be completed until 1980. Afterwards there will remain the task of keeping all the maps up to date as new roads and houses are built.

The surveyors of today are still making the large-scale maps (there are now about 150,000 of them), as their predecessors were in the nineteenth century, but the methods they use have greatly changed. The most important of these changes is the use now made of air photographs. A photograph of the ground taken from the air is not a map, because

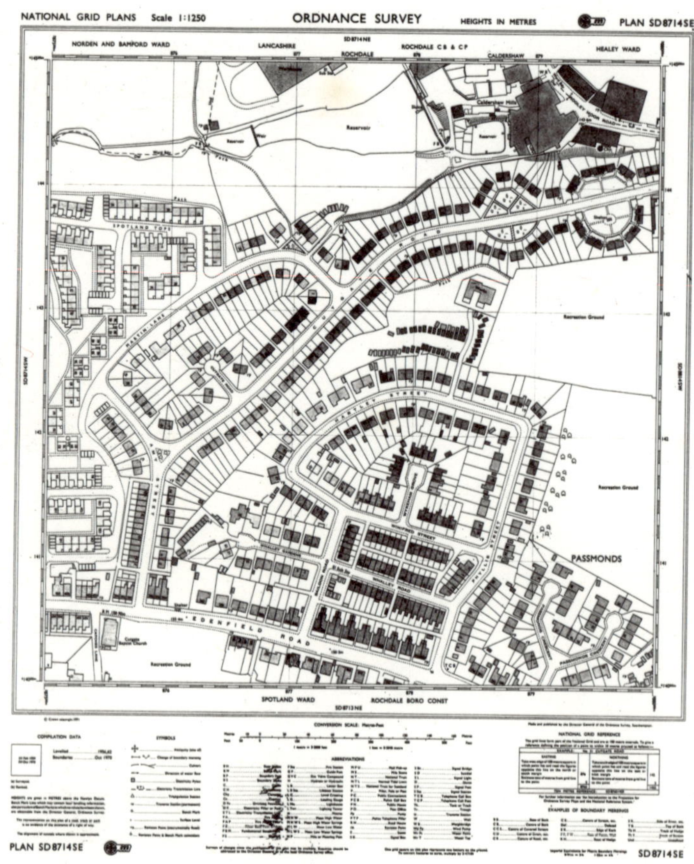

Part of a modern large-scale map (1:1250 scale – about 50 inches to one mile, 1 unit on the map equalling 1,250 units on the ground)

ısually the scale is not the ame over the whole photograph; for example, the high ground is at a larger scale than he low ground. But by using special plotting machines a nap can be made from air photographs, which, overlapping, can produce a three-limensional image when viewed through a binocular system. Another great change has resulted from the invention of new instruments for measuring listances very quickly and accurately. These instruments neasure the time taken by a ight wave (or a radio wave) to ravel to a distant point and to be reflected (or retransmitted) back again to the measuring nstrument. Because the speed of light (or radio waves) is known, the distance can be calculated. In this way distances of fifty km or more can be measured to an accuracy of a few centimetres. One of these instruments is the Tellurometer, an illustration of which appears on page 28.

In the drawing office and the printing shop a similar revolution has taken place. The draughtsmen, who have the task not only of drawing the large-scale maps produced by the surveyors but also of making from them all the smaller scales such as the two-and-a-half-inch and the one-inch maps, are using new tools and working on new materials. The printers no longer have to rely on the slow process of making prints from engraved copper plates but use fast rotary machines capable of printing many thousands of copies an hour.

Since 1791 there have been many changes, but we like to think that the spirit of the early surveyors and draughtsmen is still alive even though they no longer have to walk thirty miles a day to prove it!

Shell Pendants

Walter J. Smith shows you a new way of making them

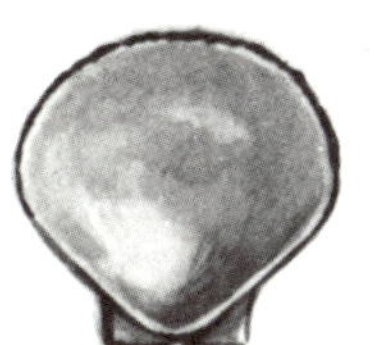

Seashells are great fun to gather and use. They can be used in various ways for ornamentation. Here is a rather different method for making pendants and necklaces out of them.

Take one of those "twirly" type of shells and grind one side away on a roughish piece of glasspaper or with a broad metal file. Stop when you reach halfway; turn the shell over and grind away the other side until the middle is about .6cm (¼″) thick.

Shell-grinding is quite fascinating. As the shell grinds away you get a perfect view of its structure. When you have finished, of course, you have mainly holes left!

If you like, you can paint your ornament with gold or silver paint, but it looks very well just as it is.

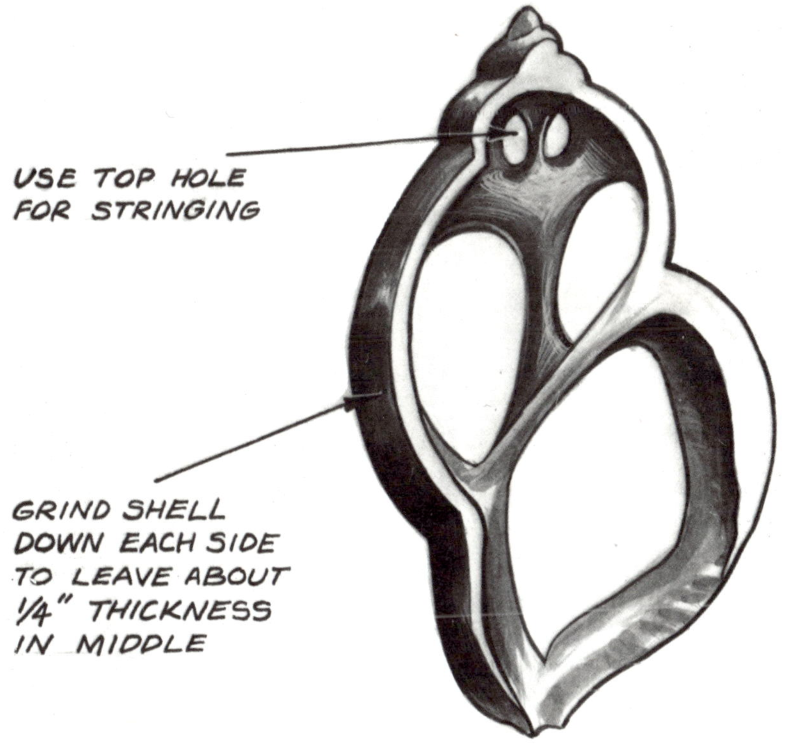

A challenge to make dampers is enjoyed by these Guides of the 2nd Maidenhead Company (St. Luke's) at camp near Chipping Norton

Badges and Challenges

Patrol Leader Claire Hodgson ta over the controls of one of the engines

Visually handicapped Guides of the 3rd Starbeck Company take their test for the Junior Red Cross certificate

Litter Nightmare

by Marcia M. Armitage

I dreamed I was climbing a mountain of tins,
Made by people who ignored litter-bins.
From the top I could see, stretching miles all around,
Old mattresses, cycles, littering the ground.
An ocean of paper hid trees from my view;
In place of the flowers were rags of each hue.
There were bottles and bones, there were old pots and pans,
There was plastic and polythene, kettles and cans.
As I gazed I grew dizzy; what could be the matter?
I fell down the mountain with a clang and a clatter.
I woke up to find I was crying in fear.
Please don't let my dream be reality here!
Look after our country with pride and with care,
And if you see litter, please don't leave it there!

The Telltale Picture

by Murray Collier

"Why I should suffer so that you can get your Photographer badge I don't know. I'm as stiff as a board," Karen grumbled, shifting her position in her sleeping-bag.

"Hush! Something might happen at any moment," Laura whispered, in mock ferocity. "You didn't have to come, you know; you could have been tucked up with the rest of the Patrol, getting your beauty sleep—and that's something you should never miss!"

Karen started to giggle, then buried her head in her sleeping-bag until she had controlled herself. The two girls lay, fully dressed, in their bags on the edge of Hornsby Wood, occasionally straining their eyes towards a darker patch of ground between two trees about ten yards in front of them. The bright moonlight glinted on a camera mounted on a tripod in front of Laura.

She, too, was finding the task of lying on her stomach extremely uncomfortable, especially as she had to keep raising herself to peer through the viewfinder of the camera. Although the tripod was closed right down until it was only nine inches high, it was still just too far above Laura's eye-level for easy viewing.

"Anyway," she whispered again, when her Patrol Leader had stopped giggling, "you know it's not just for the badge; I must try out this new camera."

As she lay in the shadow of the bush where the two Guides had concealed themselves she thought of the letter her mother had given her at breakfast that morning. It was from her father, a professional photographer. He had arrived home late the night before, when Laura was asleep, and left again early that morning on a two-week assignment with an archaeological expedition to the south of France. With the letter was a package.

Honey, she read, after opening the letter eagerly, *this is the used camera I told you about. Give it a try-out this weekend. If it is any good—or, to be honest, if you are any good with it—we'll buy it. Take the film into Mr Field on Monday. He knows all about it, and if he says you have made a good job of the pictures you can keep the camera and Mummy can pay Mr Thompson for it. Incidentally, there is a film in the camera, about half-used. Mr Thompson doesn't want it back. Have a good camp and I'll see you in a fortnight. Love, Daddy.*

Another badger emerged and was followed a moment later by a cub.

The package, which Laura had opened in great excitement, contained the camera. It was a single-lens reflex, which meant that when Laura looked through the viewfinder she actually looked out through the lens of the camera and so saw exactly the picture she would be taking.

For the tenth time she raised herself on her elbows and checked the flashgun attached to the side of the camera. She peered through the viewfinder, focused on a spot just ahead of the dark area, and then froze and concentrated her gaze. Without moving her eyes she reached back and gave Karen's shoulder a quick squeeze. This time there was no need for words; the Patrol Leader knew that action was at last at hand.

The dark patch on the ground grew paler as something moved in it, and Laura knew that a badger, for the dark patch was the entrance to a set, was emerging. She heard Karen's quick but faint indrawn breath as the animal shuffled forward into the moonlight and began to sniff the air. Evidently satisfied at last—the girls were downwind of it—it turned slightly and, as though that were a signal, another badger, smaller than the first, emerged and was followed a moment later by a cub.

Both girls were enthralled by the scene, and Laura was tempted to watch for a while longer, but

Laura led Karen out of the glare of the lights.

all three animals were grouped together, sniffing the air, and she knew that she was unlikely to get another picture as well composed. Gripping the cable release between two fingers, she depressed the end of it with her thumb.

The brilliance of the flash drove away all the shadows for less than a second, and the two Guides had the picture of the animal group frozen on the retina of their eyes. Then the darkness was back, darker still after the flash despite the bright moonlight, and the badgers were gone, moving so fast that neither girl saw them go.

Karen stretched her stiff body and then dragged herself out of her sleeping-bag. "I hate to admit it," she said, "but it was worth it, after all. Come on! Let's get back."

Gathering up their bags, groundsheets and photographic gear, they stumbled back to the tent, where the remainder of the Patrol slumbered peacefully if a trifle noisily.

The remainder of the weekend was spent in the usual enjoyable camp activities, and Laura used up the remainder of the thirty-six exposures on the film, taking what she hoped were some good shots to prove to her father that she could handle the new camera.

She slept late on Monday, the day after the return from camp, but soon after breakfast was on the way to call for Karen, her precious film in her handbag. The older girl had "been up for hours", which meant, according to her mother, about thirty minutes. She was eager to accompany Laura to the photographer's studio where the film would be processed, never having seen a studio before. Laura was quite capable of developing and printing her own films in her father's darkroom at home, but she knew that her father wanted Mr Field's expert opinion on the results from the new camera.

Laura had been to the photographer's studio on many occasions, but the scene never failed to fascinate her and she was amused to see her Patrol Leader's wide eyes as they walked through.

"Hello, Laura!" the receptionist greeted her. "Mr Field is expecting you. Go right through."

Laura led the way out of the smart reception office into the back of the building, which was a converted warehouse. They picked their way through an unbelievable clutter of spotlights, camera tripods and theatrical "props" until they came to an area which had been cleared by everything being pushed back to the walls. A large roll of coloured paper, twelve feet wide, was suspended from the ceiling and draped down to the floor. In front of it was a colourful garden-chair in which reclined a girl in a bikini, sipping at a tall glass containing a refreshing-looking golden liquid.

She saw Laura and smiled, then nodded at the glass: "Cold tea," she murmured.

Laura laughed, having seen many such scenes staged for advertisements.

Karen whispered: "It isn't really, is it?" as they edged past.

"Oh, yes it is," Laura assured her. "It's supposed to be the latest golden wine from the south of France, I expect. Who said a photo can't lie?"

Then Laura led Karen out of the glare of the lights and into the semi-gloom of the processing rooms.

"Hello, young Laura! Who's your friend?"

They turned to see John Field peering at them round a black curtain, his glasses pushed up onto his forehead.

Laura introduced Karen and handed over her film. The photographer took them into his darkroom while he inserted the film in a developing tank and started the processing.

"That will be ready in about half an hour," he said. "In the meantime you can make some coffee."

Laura laughed and nodded.

By the time the coffee was made and the staff had gathered on one of the sets to drink it, the first model gratefully exchanging the thick mug of coffee for her glass of cold tea, the film had been developed and washed. John Field examined it critically.

"Looks pretty good to me," he said. "Might even give you a job when you're older – you make the best coffee in the studio!"

This was an old joke to Laura. She, too, examined the negatives, and Mr Field promised to make prints from them if she cared to return that afternoon. Karen was particularly eager, the glamour of the studio having taken hold of her, so after lunch the two girls met again and returned to see the results of Laura's work.

The badger photograph had turned out well, and even John Field dropped his bantering manner for once to congratulate her. There was also a good one of Karen falling off the diving-board into the camp swimming-pool, but Karen was not pleased with the undignified pose. Mr Field, winking at Laura, said he thought she had distinct modelling abilities, and to her delight took some "model type" pictures of her on one of the sets.

On the bus on the way home they examined the prints more closely.

"What are those?" Karen asked, pointing to a batch at the bottom.

Laura looked at them. "They must have been the ones Mr Thompson took. Look, they are all different views of Hornsby

Monastery. You can see the Guide camp in the background."

The ruins of the monastery were on the edge of their campsite. Laura could appreciate the quality of the photographs.

"Look! He was trying out different compositions and textures," she explained to Karen. "See, from this angle all the ruins seem to point upwards, like . . ."

"Gravestones," Karen suggested.

"What a ghoulish idea!" Laura shuddered. "Still, I suppose you're right, especially in that light. Look at this one! It looks a proper haunted house, doesn't it?"

In the picture there were long shadows falling across a patch of smooth turf in the foreground, while the ruins seemed to brood over it with blank windows like empty eye-sockets.

"What's that?" Karen asked, pointing to a darker area near some bushes.

Before Laura could answer, the bus pulled up at their stop and they had to hurry to get off.

It was much later, as she was preparing for bed, that Laura took another look at the photograph. Then she went into her father's darkroom and brought back his powerful magnifying-glass. What she saw made her thoughtful, and she ran downstairs to the telephone and dialled Karen's number.

"Hello, Mrs Dixon!" she said, when the call was answered. "It's Laura. Is Karen still up?"

"Hello, my dear! Yes, she's still up and glued to the television. There's some sort of fashion parade on. This is the first time she's shown any interest; it must be that photographer friend of yours that did it."

Karen came to the phone, and Laura explained about the photograph and how she had used the magnifying-glass.

"Well, just what does it look like, that shadow?" Karen asked.

"A trapdoor," Laura told her, still examining the print.

"A trapdoor!" Karen echoed. "What would a trapdoor be doing out there? It must be a flagstone, just tilted up."

"Well, it could be," Laura admitted, "but there seems to be a step underneath it, as far as I can see. Anyway, you remember we played that stalking game round there over the weekend and there was no trapdoor open then. I think Mr Thompson took these shots earlier in the week."

"Well, we wanted something to do for the rest of the holiday," Karen said, "so here's a start. We'll visit the monastery tomorrow."

The next morning the Patrol Leader arrived at Laura's house in uniform. She carried a small rucsac in which she'd put some

The palm of her hand was covered in thick, sticky blood.

food for the day and a Primus stove.

"I thought we might spend the day on the camp-site," she explained.

They cycled out to the site and left their bikes and rucsacs at the warden's lodge while they made their investigation. Laura had the photograph with her. The new camera, now officially hers after a phone call from Mr Field to her mother, was slung round her neck. They positioned themselves so that they were viewing the ruins from the same perspective as the photograph and then walked slowly forward.

"There's nothing here," Laura said, disappointedly.

"Well, we haven't really looked yet," Karen pointed out, sensibly. "Come on! A close investigation is called for in the best Sherlock Holmes' manner."

The ground was covered with longish grass, which still showed some of the signs of their weekend stalking game. Karen got down on her knees to examine the surface more closely, while Laura took a photograph of her.

"Here! There's something under here!" Karen said.

Laura also dropped to her knees and began to feel around. Certainly there appeared to be an edge of stone, and her hand began to trace a deep, straight channel in the turf. Together they followed it until they had located a rectangle.

"Well, you were right," Karen said, rising to her feet and looking down at her friend. "The question is, how to open it?" She stopped and looked more closely at the kneeling Guide. "Laura, is something the matter?"

For a moment the younger girl didn't move; then she raised a white face to her Patrol Leader and extended a shaking hand.

"Oh, Karen," she whispered. "Look!"

The palm of her hand was covered in thick, sticky blood.

For a moment Karen stood open-mouthed, then, as Laura gave a shudder and pulled out a handkerchief to scrub frantically at her hand, she knelt beside her.

"Where did you get that? Have you cut yourself?" she asked, striving to keep her voice steady.

Laura shook her head and pointed to where their hands had traced the channel in the turf. "It's not mine – I got it from there. I thought it was mud. Oh, Karen, what are we going to do?"

"Nothing here," the Patrol Leader said, standing up. "Come on – back to the warden's lodge."

With a shaken Laura, Karen led the way back, only to find that the warden had gone out.

"Right!" said Karen decisively. "Are you feeling fit to ride? It's the police-station for us."

Laura felt better as soon as they had left the ruins behind. Ten minutes later, when they pulled up outside the police-station and dismounted, she was feeling almost her old self.

Karen led the way in, mentally rehearsing the correct manner to make a report to the police.

"Well, miss, what can I do for you?" the desk sergeant asked as the two Guides hesitated in the doorway.

Karen drew a deep breath and moved forward. "My name is Karen Dixon and this is Laura Fell," she said, clearly, and then went on to tell their story.

Laura produced the photograph and also, with another shudder, her bloodstained handkerchief.

The policeman's smile faded at the sight of it and then he looked up at a sudden movement behind the girls. A man in plain clothes moved forward and picked up the handkerchief and sniffed it.

"I heard most of it," he told the sergeant. "Get a car round for me, will you, Bill? I think we'll take a look at this place; it might clear up a few mysteries."

"You don't want us to go back there, do you?" Laura shrank away from him at the thought.

"Well, I do, actually," he admitted, then seeing the look on Laura's face, he continued, "but to set your mind at rest, I don't expect to find a body beneath that stone. Now, how about it?"

Reluctantly the two Guides agreed to return. After putting their cycles and rucsacs in the station yard they joined the detective, Inspector Swanson, in a police-car, and in a few moments were back at the monastery.

Laura had regained her confidence in the presence of the tall policeman, and when the area of the trapdoor had been pointed out she stood back and took pictures of the police at work.

It wasn't long before the flagstone was located and pulled up on end. Below it was a dark hole with steps leading down. Karen wrinkled her nose at the smell that came out. Inspector Swanson got a flashlight from the car and cautiously descended into the depths. After a moment he called out, and the driver of the car, a police-constable, reached down into the hole and brought up a bundle passed up from below. Karen and Laura gasped at the bloody mass that was laid on the ground.

"It's—it's a sheepskin!" Laura breathed at last, in relief. Then her mood changed to indignation. "Who could have done such a horrible thing?"

"Sheep-stealers," the detective said, emerging gratefully from the hole and wiping his bloodstained hands on the grass. "There have been raids on farms in the area every night during the past week and until you found this we hadn't a clue. They obviously bring the animals here and skin them, then probably take the meat away in a van."

"They must have been here last night, then," Karen pointed out, "or that blood would have dried, even though it was in the earth."

The detective nodded. "And if they try it tonight we'll be ready for them. They can't continue the game here much longer, though—there is only a small stone room down there and it is almost filled with sheepskins already."

"But how did anybody know about the secret room?" Laura asked.

Inspector Swanson shrugged. "It's probably no great secret. The Ministry of Works, who administer the ruins, probably know of it but prefer not to let the general public know; otherwise there might be an accident."

He looked thoughtful for a moment, then continued, "I seem to remember that there was a part-time keeper here up to a few months ago. He was sacked for dishonesty or something, I believe."

Karen nodded. "A Mr Barton; a surly chap he was, always complaining."

The inspector nodded. "I'll have him looked up. Now we must replace this trapdoor and make it look untouched."

"One thing puzzles me," Karen said. "If the trapdoor was open in the evening, as shown in that photo, how was it nobody spotted it during the day? There are usually some visitors around."

A moment later the area was ablaze with light.

Laura had been examining the photograph carefully again and gave a sudden exclamation. "This picture wasn't taken in the evening—it was early morning. Look, the shadows are pointing the wrong way!"

"Was it now?" Inspector Swanson said, thoughtfully. "That could be significant. Perhaps your Mr—what's his name?—Thompson—disturbed the villains. I'd better have a word with him; he might know something that could help. What's his address?"

Laura told him.

"Thanks," said the Inspector. "You've been a great help."

"We'll cycle out here tonight," Laura confided to Karen as they cycled home from the police-station.

"We'll be in at the death, eh? Do you think Inspector Swanson will let us?"

Laura chuckled. "He won't know, will he?"

"I seem to spend my time at

night in the middle of nowhere with you," Karen whispered, later that night.

The two Guides, clad warmly in thick sweaters, anoraks and jeans, left their bikes and made their way stealthily towards the monastery grounds. The moon had already risen, and even the old monastery looked picturesque in its beams.

"Careful now," Karen whispered, "or the police might hear us and send us packing."

"Or arrest us as sheep-stealers," Laura responded, with a whispered laugh.

Then she calmed down and followed her Patrol Leader's example of moving close to the ground and pushing small twigs out of the way in case they cracked.

They crawled to the top of a rise situated above the trapdoor and edged forward until they could peer cautiously over. There was no sign of the police, but from their elevated position they could see a long, dark shape behind some of the trees. It was a police-car, they guessed, and not visible from ground-level.

Karen put her mouth close to Laura's ear. "Slide under that bush to your left," she breathed. "We might be spotted against the sky otherwise. Let's get settled down."

Laura nodded and they eased themselves under the bush. Laura placed the camera with its flash-gun in front of her. Resting her chin on her two fists, she prepared to wait.

"Something's happening," Karen whispered after what seemed hours.

Laura listened. Karen was right! There was the sound of a vehicle approaching along the lane to the ruins, and a few seconds later a van, lights dimmed, pulled into the area below them.

Several figures jumped out, and while two opened the rear doors two others approached the trapdoor and raised it. They started to descend into the room below, but a whistle shrilled suddenly from the darkness and a moment later the area was ablaze with light from the headlights of the hidden car and from powerful torches.

"Stand where you are! We are police-officers," a man shouted, and all was confusion as the sheep-stealers milled about uncertainly and police-officers raced in among them.

The driver's door of the van opened quietly and a man slipped cautiously out. He made his way to the foot of the slope where the girls lay, then his nerve broke and he made a mad dash for freedom.

The two Guides had risen to their feet and stood frozen in his path. As he pounded over the crest of the slope, Laura thrust her camera forward and pressed the shutter release. The sudden blinding flash a few feet in front of him unnerved the fugitive and he threw up his hands to his eyes, gave a despairing cry and stumbled back to trip and roll down the slope to the feet of a pursuing policeman.

"Who's that up there?" demanded the voice of Inspector Swanson.

The two girls descended the slope cautiously, uncertain of their reception.

"What the heck are you two doing here?" the detective demanded, as soon as he recognised them.

"Er—just looking on," Karen said, sheepishly.

"Lucky they were, sir," the policeman holding the fugitive interposed. "This one would have got away."

The two girls flashed him a grateful smile, and then Laura saw an answering smile twitch the corners of the inspector's mouth.

"Did you learn anything from Mr Thompson?" she asked, quickly.

"We certainly did," was the reply. "He'd already taken some pictures with his other camera, and one of them showed the van in the bushes. We were able to get the number, and we knew who our villains were even before they turned up tonight. Mr Thompson disturbed them one morning last week and they had to hide until he had gone before they could close the trapdoor."

"Well, they say that every picture tells a story," Karen laughed. "These certainly did!"

And Laura, thinking of the picture she had taken up on the slope when she had pressed the shutter-release in sheer fright, and of the story she would tell her father, agreed happily.

Chasing the Blues

by Eileen Chivers

Said Annabella, "I'm all right–
School uniform is blue."
Groaned Janet, "Mine is green and white.
Oh, what am I to do?
Mum can't afford to buy, besides
Blue shorts and tee shirts just for Guides."

Young Joan was sitting quietly,
Not joining in the wails,
But then she jumped up suddenly
And shouted "Jumble sales!"
The other Robins raised their eyes
And looked at her in great surprise.

"You can't wear that," the C.A. cried,
In tones of deepest sorrow.
"In that case," thought the newest Guide,
"I'm going home tomorrow.
My tee shirt's red, but my poor mother
Can't afford to buy another."

Inspection done, the C.A. went;
The Guides began to chatter;
The Robins gathered in their tent
To talk about the matter
Of getting in the proper gear
To wear at camp the following year.

"But can we run one on our own?"
"I really rather doubt it."
"I don't mean that at all," said Joan.
"Let me explain about it.
At jumble sales you don't just sell.
You have to buy the things as well.

"I've helped my Mum with many such,
Run by the Ladies' Guild.
With things that don't cost very much
The stalls are always filled,
And lots of bargains can be found
By those who care to look around."

From that time forth the Robins sought
For every sale they could.
Blue shorts and cardigans they bought,
And jumpers cheap and good.
Tee shirts white and tee shirts blue—
Some of them as good as new.

They washed and pressed and did repairs
On what they had acquired,
Sewed buttons on and mended tears
And darned things if required.
They also had a dyeing session,
Which made a very great impression.

The Camp Adviser came once more.
Loud were her exclamations.
Perceiving what the Robins wore,
She cried, "Congratulations!"
The cheerful Robins made reply,
"We joined the Guides to do or dye!"

Put on your own Pantomime

Doris Bellringer, an Amateur Producer, Gives Help and Hints

Produce a pantomime within a few days of Christmas, and your audience, at least, is no problem. Most mothers are frantically searching for an inexpensive way of keeping their younger children amused until school begins again. This timing, however, poses a problem as the few weeks immediately preceding Christmas are usually very busy with school activities, and you have little time for rehearsals.

It is, therefore, advisable to make a start as early as August and even before this. In fact, it is an excellent idea to keep a notebook in which you record suitable jokes (from comics, TV, radio or other sources) and also odd snatches of conversation. This material will often suggest scenes or interludes in the pantomime. During the summer holidays call a meeting of the keenest performers. Ask them to bring paper, pencil, a packed lunch and plenty of ideas. Incidentally, the title of the pantomime should have been chosen before this and agreed by the performers. There are on the market many scripted pantomimes both basic and adapted which can be used if time is short, but it is certainly more fun to write one's own.

Before the script-writing meeting the producer, director and script co-ordinator (which is you) should buy a version of the fairy story and break this down into ten or twelve situations. Pen and paper should be provided for those who have forgotten to bring them. Two or three Guides will probably want to collaborate, and they should be provided with a "situation" and asked to write the dialogue. They will probably want to read their own efforts and—as the writing is usually indecipherable—this is a good idea. It is well to approve of everything at this stage and pass quickly to a second batch of "situations". If these can be tackled before lunch you are doing well. After lunch the working atmosphere tends to deteriorate and very little more "serious" writing will be done.

If you—as producer—listen carefully to the general chat you will be provided with quite a lot of extra material. Nothing suggested should be turned down out of hand. However outrageous it appears, it may contain the germ of an idea, and the writers should be sent home convinced that this pantomime will be the best ever.

The cast of "Snow White and the Seven Dwarfs"

Now comes the task of getting a workable script from the copious notes. Do insist that all writing should be left with you. The plea to take it home and finish it should be resisted; you will probably not get it back. Make the point that this is very valuable material and any further contributions will be welcome. From now on you are on your own. Try not to discard too much. Your task will be chiefly to make additions in order to keep the story-line. It is important to do this if your audience is

Guides of the 4th Hayes (Kent) Company and Brownies of the 3rd Hayes Pack rehearse their adaptation of the pantomime "Snow White and the Seven Dwarfs"

to consist of small children who have probably been told the story many times. It is also important to the cast that you do not cut the jokes.

When the script is finished it will be received by the cast as "our pantomime" and rehearsals will go with a swing. Casting can cause much heartache and may be done in many different ways, most of which are very time-consuming. I have found the simplest and probably the most effective is to make a list of the characters with a short description against each and a note to indicate whether the speaking part is large, medium or small. Give a copy to each members of the cast and ask her to list the three characters she would wish to play. Surprisingly, this quite frequently results in a good, quick and efficient casting system.

It is a mistake to start rehearsals too early and very easy to leave them too late. Guides, when keen, are often excellent actors, but they soon get bored, and learning lines presents problems to some. Ad-libbing is a tricky question. It is, of course, essential in an emergency, but does tend to throw other performers out, and if, say, the first courtier is deprived of one of her lines it may seem to her to be a real tragedy. It is therefore a great help to enlist the help of a sympathetic adult to act as prompter.

At the dress rehearsal, which should be as soon as possible after Christmas, you must be prepared for quite a few of the cast not to appear. If an excuse is sent it should be accepted, and everyone will hope that the actor will arrive for the performance. If no message is received it may be necessary to rearrange the cast. This leads to complications. A year or two ago we produced Snow White and the Seven Dwarfs, but were down to four dwarfs for the dress rehearsal. The cast was rearranged to give us six dwarfs, two of whom studied parts for a whole afternoon and became practically word-perfect. At the first performance we did, in fact, have eight dwarfs, but this provided the headline in the local paper GIRL GUIDES PRODUCE EXTRA DWARF FOR SNOW WHITE.

ANSWERS TO PUZZLES

Morse Code Crossword (p. 30)

1a and 3a	B-P, Founder of Scouts and Guides
12a, 13a, 2d	SOS, Distress signal
18d, 20a, 1d	CHQ, London headquarters of the Girl Guides Association
16d, 6a	PL, Patrol Leader
7d, 23a, 11a	WHO, World Health Organisation
21a, 10d, 8a	USA, United States of America
14d, 5a	OK, Meaning "all right" or "agreed"
4d, 19a	LS, Initials shown on the Life Saver badge
9, 22a	TV, Television
17a, 15	NE, North-east

Find the Flowers (p. 33): 1. bluebell, 2. forget-me-not, 3. honesty, 4. red-hot poker, 5. thyme, 6. stock, 7. burning bush, 8. thrift, 9. Canterbury bell, 10. iris, 11. rose.

Bird Crossword (p. 33): *Across:* bob-a-job, sausages, oil, urn, yell, seaside, apple, warm, earn, tin, set, one. *Down:* log, was, zoo, rug, bad, bed, bill, streams, me, us, nap, nil, he, yarn, spot, deed, pane, windy, to

Coin Quiz (p. 33)

All About Anne (p. 50): 1-banned, 2-canned, 3-planned, 4-banner, 5-annexe, 6-fanned, 7-manned, 8-tanned, 9-Cannes, 10-panned.

EXPLORING THE ARTS (p. 51)

Objects: 1-Stencilling, 2-whittling, 3-ballet, 4-spatter prints, 5-clay modelling, 6-rushwork, 7-embroidery, 8-lettering, 9-straw work, 10-handbell ringing, 11-music, 12-weaving.

Art: 1-Canada, 2-Egypt; 3-Japan, 4-Africa, 5-Greece, 6-Ireland, 7-Italy, 8-Iran.

Books: 1-Burnett, *The Secret Garden*; 2-Emily Brontë, *Wuthering Heights*; 3-Eliot, *The Mill on the Floss*; 4-Stevenson, *Child's Garden of Verses*; 5-Beecher-Stowe, *Uncle Tom's Cabin*; 6-Dickens, *David Copperfield*; 7-Grahame, *The Wind in the Willows*; 8-Scott, *The Lady of the Lake*; 9-Molesworth, *The Cuckoo Clock*; 10-Kipling, *Just So Stories*; 11-Carroll, *Alice Through the Looking-glass*; 12-Austen, *Pride and Prejudice.*

Drama: 1-Mexico, 2-Japan, 3-Netherlands, 4-America, 5-Scotland, 6-India, 7-Spain, 8-Jordan, 9-Turkey.

S.O.S. (p. 50)

S.O.S. S.O.S. Please rescue me my boat has drifted away

Pathfinder Puzzle (p. 50)

1. Prepared	6. Indians
2. Ass	7. Nose
3. Trail	8. Dream
4. Hangers	9. Edinburgh
5. Flag	10. Rudder

BECOMING A HOMEMAKER (p. 49)

Tools: 1-Mend a fuse in fuse-box, 2-clear blocked sink, 3-new washer on tap, 4-drive in a screw, 5-hang curtains, 6-replace fuse in a plug, 7-turn off water at main, 8-paint walls.

Untidy Room: 1-Replace pelmet on rail, 2-mend torn curtain, 3-wash dirty windows, 4-remove cobweb, 5-straighten picture, 6-water flowers, 7-wipe up spilt liquid, 8-empty ashtray, 9-mend or rebind frayed flex, 10-pick up cores and empty wastepaper bin, 11-tidy up newspapers, 12-open window to air room.

Hostess: Take coat on arrival; ask visitor if she takes milk, sugar, likes early-morning tea (or coffee); turn down bed, place in hot bottle (or warm with electric blanket); put extra blanket out in case required; biscuits and water at bedside; books to read; provide coat-hangers, soap and towel, flowers to cheer the room.

Cooking: 1-Shepherd's pie-G; 2-bacon and egg-E; 3-scrambled eggs-A; 4-fruit cake-H; 5-small tea-cakes-C; 6-stew-D; 7-sponge cake -B; 8-poached eggs-F.

Flower Quiz (pp. 64, 65)

1-poppy *(papaver rhoeas)*, worn on Remembrance Day because poppies were among the first wild-flowers to bloom on the battlefields of Flanders after World War 1. *Colour picture No. 1.*

2-gorse (whin or furze) (*ulex Europaeus*). This shrub blooms all the year round, so kissing is never out of season. *Colour picture No. 2.*

3-Hyacinth was killed by a quoit blown off course by Zephyrus. The wild hyacinth or bluebell *(Endymion non-scriptus)* is quite different from the "Bluebells of Scotland" or harebells. *Colour picture No. 3.*

4-mustard *(brassica nigra). Colour picture No. 4.*

5-the common daisies *(bellis perennis).*

6-the primrose *(primula vulgaris)* flowers on banks and in woods. *Photo "A" on page 64.*

7-marsh marigold or kingcup *(caltha palustris). Colour picture No. 5.*

8-St. David's Day, and the daffodil is the national flower of Wales. *Photo "B" on page 64.*

ENJOYING THE OUT-OF-DOORS (p. 52)

Trees: Oak: 4-buds, 6-leaves, 10-seeds; Elm: 2-buds, 7-leaves, 11 seeds; Ash: 3-buds, 8-leaves, 9-seeds; Sycamore; 1-bud, 5-leaves, 12-seeds.

Outdoor Activities: 1-Bridge: round turn and two half-hitches, clove-hitch, anchor-bend; 2-Climbing: bowline; 3-Riding: highwayman's hitch; 4-Ladder: round turn and two half-hitches, clovehitch or marlin-spike hitch; 5-Boating: round turn and two half-hitches

Signalling: *Semaphore* — GREAT BEAR IS ALSO CALLED THE PLOUGH. Missing letters: E, A, L, L, E, G. *Morse*— CAN YOU FIND THE NORTH AT NIGHT?

Map symbols: ON ORDNANCE SURVEY MAPS.

1-Site of battle, 2-windmill in use, 3-Youth Hostel, 4-civil airport, 5-lighthouse, 6-post-office, 7-marsh-land, 8-wood, 9-level crossing, 10-tunnel, 11-trunk or 'A' road, 12-'B' road, 13-minor road, 14-county boundary, 15-parish boundary.

From a Guider's Notebook

Guides and Brownies celebrate Thinking Day, which is February 22nd each year, the joint birthday of Lord and Lady Baden-Powell. How about an annual Thanking Day, on which we all express gratitude for the year's blessings —especially, perhaps, for all that Guiding does for us and for youth all over the world? It's an idea! The Americans keep an annual Thanksgiving Day each November. We could well follow suit in this country.

Maori "Pois" Action Song. An unusual Thinking Day activity I came across was performed by the 2nd Munster Guide Company in Germany. The Guides made Maori-type dresses and head-bands, as the photograph by their Guider, Mrs P. Knight, shows. They performed with "pois", which are balls on string, originally designed to develop eye and finger coordination. The Guides made their "pois" from paper, string and old stockings. They learned the actions and did them to a traditional Maori tune.

From Singapore. I read about an interesting Guide camp in Singapore. On Visitors' Day each Patrol carried out a Challenge—decoding and carrying a message, decorating a bird-tree, making a picture from grasses and an object from natural wood.

One of the highlights of the camp was a sunrise hike by Guides, who set off at 5.30 a.m. and had to be back in camp by 8 a.m. Between these hours they cooked themselves breakfast.

Titbits to Make. Stuffed dates make a tasty novelty. Make neat slits in the sides of dates and take out the stones. Slip an almond or half a walnut into the space left by the stone. Roll the dates in icing sugar. Delicious!

To make peppermint creams, beat up the white of an egg in a dessertspoonful of water and one teaspoonful of essence of peppermint. Stir in most of 1lb of icing sugar, pressing all the lumps out with a spoon, until there is a nice, firm paste. Sprinkle a pastry-board with icing sugar, roll out the paste into 1cm thickness, and then stamp out into little rounds with a small pastry-cutter. Leave the sweets to dry and harden on greaseproof paper.